A SIMPLE
PRAYER BOOK

Published 2011 by the Incorporated Catholic Truth Society, 42-46 Harleyford Road, London SE11 5AY. www.ctsbooks.org. Compilation, layout, design of this edition © 2011 The Incorporated Catholic Truth Society. First compiled and published 1886, revised and reprinted from time to time, © The Incorporated Catholic Truth Society. Printed in Italy.

ISBN 978 1 86082 598 9

Nihil obstat: The Reverend Canon John Redford S.T.L., L.S.S., D.D.
Imprimatur: ✠ Peter Smith, Archbishop of Southwark, 23 May 2011.
The Nihil obstat and Imprimatur *are a declaration that a book or pamphlet is considered to be free from doctrinal or moral error. It is not implied that those who have granted the Nihil obstat and* Imprimatur *agree with the contents, opinions or statements expressed.*

Excerpts from the English translation of *The Roman Missal* © 2010, International Commission on English in the Liturgy Corporation (ICEL); excerpts from the English translation of The Liturgy of the Hours © 1974, ICEL; excerpts from the English translation of *Holy Communion & Worship of the Eucharist outside Mass* © 1974, ICEL; excerpt from the English translation of *Rite of Penance* © 1974, ICEL. All rights reserved. Latin text © Libreria Editrice Vaticana, Vatican City State, 2008. *Concordat cum originali*: Martin Foster (England and Wales). Permission granted for distribution in the dioceses of Scotland.

Front cover image: design © 2010 The Incorporated Catholic Truth Society.

Page 6: The Virgin and Child with SS. Anne and John the Baptist, c.1499 (charcoal, chalk on paper) (see detail 99053), Vinci, Leonardo da (1452-1519)/ National Gallery, London, UK. Page 32: Crucifixion by Guilio Campi © Alexander Burkatovski/CORBIS. Page 36: The Madonna of Loreto (pen and ink), Carracci, Annibale (1560-1609) (studio of)/Phillips, The International Fine Art Auctioneers, UK. Page 45: Hands of an Apostle, 1508 (brush drawing) (a study for an altarpiece commissioned by Jacob Heller), Durer, Albrecht (1471-1528)/Graphische Sammlung Albertina, Vienna, Austria. Page 56: Christ at Emmaus by Jan de Beer © Burstein Collection/CORBIS. Page 100: Drawing of an Angel by Andrea del Sarto © Alinari Archives/CORBIS. Page 110: The Eucharist (oil on panel), Kessel, Jan van, the Elder (1626-79)/Private Collection, Rafael Valls Gallery, London, UK/www.bridgeman.co.uk.

A SIMPLE PRAYER BOOK

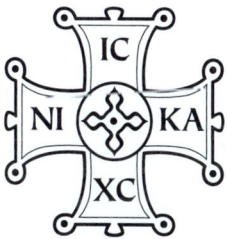

*All booklets are published
thanks to the generosity of the supporters
of the Catholic Truth Society*

A Simple Prayer Book

Prayers & Devotions

Basic Prayers 7

Morning and Evening Prayer 9
- **Morning Prayer** 9
- **During the Day** 13
  - The Angelus 13
- **Evening Prayer** 14

Prayers to the Holy Spirit 19

Penitential Prayers 22
- **Sacrament of Reconciliation** 22
- **Examination of Conscience** 24
- **Going to Confession** 29
- **The Way of The Cross** 31

Prayers to Our Lady 37
- **The Holy Rosary** 37
- **Litany of the Blessed Virgin Mary** 39

Prayers for Various Needs and Occasions 42
- Act of Faith, Hope and Charity 42
- For the Faithful Departed 43
- Prayer of Saint Ignatius 45
- Prayer to Saint Michael 46
- In Temptation 47
- Prayer for the Pope 48
- Prayer for Vocations 49
- Prayer for Peace 50

Prayer before a Crucifix 51
A Night Prayer 52
The Divine Mercy 53

THE EUCHARIST

THE ORDER OF MASS 57
  The Introductory Rites 57
  The Liturgy of the Word 62
  The Liturgy of the Eucharist 68
  The Communion Rite 90
  The Concluding Rites 95

IF YOU CANNOT ATTEND MASS 96
  Spiritual Communion 96

PRAYERS FOR HOLY COMMUNION 98
  Before Holy Communion 98
  After Holy Communion 102

RITE OF EUCHARISTIC EXPOSITION AND BENEDICTION . 105
  A Quarter Hour Before the Blessed Sacrament 111

CATHOLIC TEACHING

SUMMARY OF CHRISTIAN DOCTRINE 115
  The Mass Simply Explained 120
  The Sunday Obligation 122
  Fasting and Abstinence 123
  Note on Indulgences 124

PRAYERS & DEVOTIONS
Basic Prayers

Our Father

Our Father, who art in heaven, hallowed be thy name. Thy Kingdom come. Thy will be done on earth as it is in heaven. Give us this day our daily bread, and forgive us our trespasses, as we forgive those who trespass against us, and lead us not into temptation, but deliver us from evil. Amen.

Hail Mary

Hail, Mary, full of grace, the Lord is with thee. Blessed art thou among women, and blessed is the fruit of thy womb, Jesus. Holy Mary, Mother of God, pray for us sinners, now, and at the hour of our death. Amen.

Glory be to the Father

Glory be to the Father, and to the Son, and to the Holy Spirit. As it was in the beginning, is now, and ever shall be, world without end. Amen.

I Believe (The Apostles' Creed)

I believe in God,
the Father almighty,
Creator of heaven and earth,

and in Jesus Christ, his only Son, our Lord,
who was conceived by the Holy Spirit,
born of the Virgin Mary,
suffered under Pontius Pilate,
was crucified, died and was buried;
he descended into hell;
on the third day he rose again from the dead;
he ascended into heaven,
and is seated at the right hand of God the Father almighty;
from there he will come to judge the living and the dead.

I believe in the Holy Spirit,
the holy catholic Church,
the communion of saints,
the forgiveness of sins,
the resurrection of the body,
and life everlasting.
Amen.

Morning and Evening Prayer

Morning Prayer

V. Lord, open our lips.
R. And we shall praise your name.
    Glory be to the Father… (Alleluia)
A hymn, suitable to the time of day or feast, may follow.

Psalm 99

(*This or alternative psalms may be said*)
Cry out with joy to the Lord, all the earth
Serve the Lord with gladness.
Come before him, singing for joy.

Know that he, the Lord, is God.
He made us, we belong to him,
We are the people, the sheep of his flock.

Go within his gates, giving thanks.
Enter his courts with songs of praise.
Give thanks to him and bless his name.

Indeed, how good is the Lord,
Eternal his merciful love.
He is faithful from age to age.
    Glory be to the Father…

Scripture

(An alternative passage may be used)

You know what hour it is, how it is full time now for you to wake from sleep. The night is far gone, the day is at hand. Let us cast off the works of darkness and put on the armour of light; let us conduct ourselves becomingly as in the day. (*Rm* 13:11-13)

The Benedictus (*Lk* 1:68-79)

Blessed be the Lord, the God of Israel!
He has visited his people and redeemed them.
   He has raised up for us a mighty saviour
   in the house of David his servant,
   as he promised by the lips of holy men,
   those who were his prophets from of old.
A saviour who would free us from our foes,
from the hands of all who hate us.
So his love for our fathers is fulfilled
and his holy covenant remembered.
   He swore to Abraham our father to grant us,
   that free from fear, and saved from
   the hands of our foes,
   we might serve him in holiness and justice
   all the days of our life in his presence.

> As for you little child,
> you shall be called a prophet of God, the Most High.
> You shall go ahead of the Lord
> to prepare a way for him,
>> To make known to his people their salvation,
>> through forgiveness of all their sins,
>> the loving kindness of the heart of our God
>> who visits us like the dawn from on high.
> He will give light to those in darkness,
> those who dwell in the shadow of death,
> and guide us into the way of peace.
>> Glory be to the Father…

Intercessions

(*These or other intercessions may be used*)

Let us pray to Christ our Lord, the sun who enlightens all people –

> **Lord our Saviour, give us life!**
> (*may be repeated after each line*)
> We thank you for the gift of this new day –
> May your Holy Spirit guide us to do your will –
> Help us to manifest your love to all those we meet –
> Renew in us your gifts. May we go forth in peace –
>> Our Father…

Concluding prayer

Almighty God, you have given us this day; strengthen us with your power and keep us from falling into sin, so that whatever we say, or think, or do, may be in your service and for the sake of the kingdom.

We ask this through Christ our Lord. Amen.

☦ The Lord bless us, keep us from all evil and bring us to everlasting life. Amen.

Alternative personal prayers may include:
Our Father. Hail Mary. Glory be. I Believe.

Offering

O my God, I offer you all my thoughts, words, actions, and sufferings; and I beseech you to give me your grace that I may not offend you this day, but may faithfully serve you and do your holy will in all things. I entrust myself completely to your boundless mercy today and always.

O Lord you have brought me to the beginning of a new day. Save me by your power so that I may not fall into any sin. May everything I say, and all that I do, be directed to the performance of your justice, through Christ our Lord.

Lord, may everything I do begin with your inspiration, continue with your help and reach conclusion under your guidance.

Morning offering

O Jesus, through the most pure heart of Mary, I offer you all my prayers, thoughts, works and sufferings of this day for all the intentions of your most Sacred Heart.
O most Sacred Heart of Jesus, I place all my trust in you.
O most Sacred Heart of Jesus, I place all my trust in you.
O most Sacred Heart of Jesus, I place all my trust in you.

DURING THE DAY

The Angelus

May be said morning, noon, and night, to put us in mind that God the Son became man for our salvation.

V. The Angel of the Lord declared to Mary:
R. And she conceived of the Holy Spirit.
   Hail Mary…
V. Behold the handmaid of the Lord:
R. Be it done to me according to your word.
   Hail Mary…
V. And the Word was made flesh:
R. And dwelt among us.

Hail Mary…

V. Pray for us, O holy Mother of God.

R. That we may be made worthy of the promises of Christ.

Let us pray:

Pour forth, we beseech you, O Lord, your grace into our hearts, that we, to whom the Incarnation of Christ, your Son, was made known by the message of an Angel, may by his Passion and Cross ✠ be brought to the glory of his Resurrection, through the same Christ our Lord. **R. Amen.** (*In Eastertime, the Angelus is replaced by the Regina Caeli, page* 41).

Evening Prayer

V. O God, come to our aid.
**R. O Lord, make haste to help us.
Glory be to the Father…**

Hymn

*A hymn, suitable to the time of day or feast,
may follow, eg*:
O Trinity of blessed light,
O Unity of princely might,
The fiery sun now goes his way;
Shed thou within our hearts thy ray.

To thee our morning song of praise,
To thee our evening prayer we raise;
Thy glory suppliant we adore
For ever and for evermore.

All laud to God the Father be;
All praise, eternal Son, to thee;
All glory, as is ever meet,
To God the holy Paraclete. Amen.

Psalm 16

(*An alternative psalm may be said*)
Preserve me, God, I take refuge in you.
I say to the Lord: 'You are my God.
My happiness lies in you alone'.

He has put into my heart a marvellous love
for the faithful ones who dwell in his land.
Those who choose other gods increase their sorrows.
Never will I offer their offerings of blood.
Never will I take their name upon my lips.

O Lord, it is you who are my portion and cup;
it is you who are my prize.
The lot marked out for me is my delight:
welcome indeed the heritage that falls to me!

I will bless the Lord who gives me counsel,
who even at night directs my heart.

I keep the Lord ever in my sight:
since he is at my right hand, I shall stand firm.

And so my heart rejoices, my soul is glad;
even my body shall rest in safety.
For you will not leave my soul among the dead,
nor let your beloved know decay.

You will show me the path of life,
the fullness of joy in your presence,
at your right hand happiness for ever.
   Glory be to the Father…

Scripture

(*An alternative passage may be used*)

Let us give thanks to the God and Father of our Lord Jesus Christ, the merciful Father, the God from whom all help comes! He helps us in all our troubles, so that we are able to help those who have all kinds of troubles, using the same help that we ourselves have received from God. (2 *Co* 1:3-4)

Magnificat (*Lk* 1:46-55)

My soul glorifies the Lord,
my spirit rejoices in God, my Saviour.
He looks on his servant in her lowliness;
henceforth all ages will call me blessed.
   The Almighty works marvels for me.
   Holy his name!

His mercy is from age to age,
on those who fear him.
He puts forth his arm in strength
and scatters the proud-hearted.
He casts the mighty from their thrones
and raises the lowly.
He fills the starving with good things,
sends the rich away empty.
He protects Israel, his servant,
remembering his mercy,
the mercy promised to our fathers,
to Abraham and his sons for ever.
Glory be to the Father…

Intercessions

(These or other intercessions may be used)

May your kingdom of peace and justice be realised on earth as in heaven –

Lord, hear our prayer.

(may be repeated after each line)

Show yourself to all who seek you in sincerity of heart – Lord Jesus Christ, light of all the nations, shine upon those who walk in darkness and in the shadow of death – Be with all those who suffer in mind, body or spirit – Show mercy to the dead; bring them to rejoice in the company of the blessed Virgin Mary and all your saints –

Our Father…

Concluding prayer

Let our evening prayer rise before you like incense, Lord, and may your blessing shower down upon us: so that now and for ever your grace may heal and save us. We ask this through Christ Our Lord. Amen. ✠ May the Lord bless us, keep us from all evil and bring us to everlasting life.

Alternative personal prayers may include:
Our Father. Hail Mary. Glory be. I Believe.

O my God, I thank you for all the benefits which I have ever received from you, and especially this day. Give me light to see what sins I have committed, and grant me the grace to be truly sorry for them. (*A brief examination of conscience may follow*).

O my God, because you are so good, I am very sorry that I have sinned against you and by the help of your grace I will not sin again.

On going to bed

Into your hands, O Lord, I commend my spirit: Lord Jesus, receive my soul. In the name of our Lord Jesus Christ crucified, I lay me down to rest. Bless me, O Lord, and defend me; preserve me from a sudden and unprovided death and from all dangers, and bring me to life everlasting with you.

Prayers to the Holy Spirit

Veni Creator Spiritus

Come, Holy Spirit, Creator, come
from thy bright heavenly throne.
Come, take possession of our souls,
and make them all thy own.

    Thou who art called the Paraclete,
    best gift of God above,
    the living spring, the living fire,
    sweet unction and true love.

Thou who art sevenfold in thy grace,
finger of God's right hand;
his promise, teaching little ones
to speak and understand.

    O guide our minds with thy blest light,
    with love our hearts inflame;
    and with thy strength which never decays,
    confirm our mortal frame.

Far from us drive our deadly foe;
true peace unto us bring;
and through all perils lead us safe
beneath thy sacred wing.

    Through thee may we the Father know,
    through thee the eternal Son,
    and thee, the Spirit of them both,
    thrice-blessed Three in One.

All glory to the Father be,
with his co-equal Son;
the same to thee, great Paraclete,
while endless ages run.

Veni Sancte Spiritus

Come, Holy Spirit, come!
And from your celestial home
Shed a ray of light divine!

Come, Father of the poor!
Come, source of all our store!
Come, within our bosoms shine.

You, of comforters the best;
You, the soul's most welcome guest;
Sweet refreshment here below.

In our labour, rest most sweet;
Grateful coolness in the heat;
Solace in the midst of woe.

O most blessed Light divine,
Shine within these hearts of yours,
And our inmost being fill!

Where you are not, we have naught,
Nothing good in deed or thought,
Nothing free from taint of ill.

Heal our wounds, our strength renew;
On our dryness pour your dew;
Wash the stains of guilt away.

Bend the stubborn heart and will;
Melt the frozen, warm the chill;
Guide the steps that go astray.

On the faithful, who adore
And confess you, evermore
In your sevenfold gift descend.

Give them virtue's sure reward;
Give them your salvation, Lord;
Give them joys that never end. Amen.

Prayer to the Holy Spirit

Come, O Holy Spirit, fill the hearts of your faithful, and enkindle in them the fire of your love.

V. Send forth your Spirit and they shall be created.

R. And you shall renew the face of the earth.

Let us pray:

O God, who taught the hearts of the faithful by the light of the Holy Spirit, grant that by the gift of the same Spirit we may be always truly wise and ever rejoice in his consolation. Through Christ our Lord. **R. Amen.**

Penitential Prayers

Sacrament of Reconciliation

Remember that the sacrament is above all an act of God's love. It is a personal moment to be lived in a relationship of love with God. It is not routine, nor an ordeal to be gone through, but is very much part of the personal renewal which takes place in each person. You are invited, in the light of God's love, to recognise the sinfulness of your life, to have true sorrow for your sins, and a firm intention to avoid them in future.

Essential elements of a good confession

To make a good confession, we should:

1. Pray first, asking God to help us.
2. Make a sincere examination of conscience to see how we have sinned since our last confession.
3. Confess our sins simply, with humility and honesty.
4. Make our act of contrition with heartfelt sorrow and a "firm purpose of amendment", being determined that we will avoid the occasions of sin.
5. Devoutly carry out the penance prescribed and pray in thanksgiving for God's overflowing love and mercy.

Prayer before Confession

Almighty and merciful God,
you have brought me here in the name of your Son
to receive your mercy and grace in my time of need.
Open my eyes to see the evil I have done.
Touch my heart and convert me to yourself.
Where sin has separated me from you,
may your love unite me to you again:
where sin has brought weakness,
may your power heal and strengthen;
where sin has brought death,
may your Spirit raise to new life.
Give me a new heart to love you,
so that my life may reflect the image of your Son.
May the world see the glory
of Christ revealed in your Church,
and come to know that he is the one whom
you have sent, Jesus Christ, your Son, our Lord. Amen.

The Confiteor

I confess to almighty God and to you, my brothers and sisters, that I have greatly sinned, in my thoughts and in my words, in what I have done and in what I have failed to do, through my fault, through my fault, through my most grievous fault; therefore I ask blessed Mary ever-Virgin, all the Angels and Saints, and you, my brothers and sisters, to pray for me to the Lord our God.

An Act of Contrition

O my God, I am sorry and beg pardon for all my sins, and detest them above all things, because they deserve your dreadful punishments, because they have crucified my loving Saviour Jesus Christ, and, most of all, because they offend your infinite goodness; and I firmly resolve, by the help of your grace, never to offend you again, and carefully to avoid the occasions of sin.

EXAMINATION OF CONSCIENCE

Careful preparation is vital in order to make the most of this encounter with our loving heavenly Father. Find some time to be alone and quiet to reflect on your life, your relationship with God and others. An examination of conscience provides us with what we are going to say in the confessional. Without time given to such examination our confession is in danger of being incomplete. There are many ways: one is to use a gospel passage, especially one of the many healing miracles or occasions of forgiveness (eg Lk 15:11-32; Jn 4:5-42; Mt 18:21-35; Lk 18:9-14). Imagine you are the person being healed or forgiven by Jesus. Read the scripture passage, imagine you are in the scene, and listen to the words of Jesus. He speaks to you! What do you say? Alternatively, Jesus summed up and extended the Ten Commandments by his two great commandments (Mk 12:28-42): Love God and your neighbour.

Mortal sin is sin whose object is a grave matter and which is also committed with full knowledge and deliberate consent (*Catechism* 1857). We must confess all mortal sins. We are not obliged to confess all venial sins.

We commit venial sin when, in a less serious matter, we do not observe the standard prescribed by the moral law, or when we disobey the moral law in a grave matter, but without full knowledge or without complete consent (*Catechism* 1862). Confession of venial sins is an act of devotion. We need not be unduly anxious to confess them all, but may rather choose to focus on areas of our life that are most in need of God's grace.

The following examination of conscience can help us to measure our lives by the objective standard of Christ's teaching. We may also consider more generally how we may have failed in our lives to live fully as disciples of Christ.

Sins against God

Have I rejected my faith, refused to find out more about it?

Have I forgotten my daily prayers or said them badly?

Have I experimented with the occult or put my trust in fortune tellers or horoscopes?

Have I blasphemed against God or used bad language?

Have I shown disrespect for holy things, places or people?

Have I missed Mass on Sundays or Holydays through my own fault?

Have I let myself be distracted at Mass or distracted others?

Have I received Holy Communion in a state of mortal sin?

Have I received Holy Communion without proper reverence, care or thanksgiving?

Sins against myself and others

Have I been impatient, angry or jealous?

Have I brooded over injuries or refused to forgive?

Have I taken part in or encouraged abortion, the destruction of human embryos, euthanasia or any other means of taking human life?

Have I been verbally or physically violent to others?

Have I been racist in my thoughts, words or deeds?

Have I hurt anyone by speaking badly about them?

Have I betrayed confidences without good cause or revealed things simply to hurt others?

Have I judged others rashly?

Have I been drunk or used illegal drugs?

Have I driven dangerously or inconsiderately?

Have I spoken in an obscene way?

Have I looked at obscene pictures, films or books?

Have I been involved in any impure behaviour on my own or with someone else?

Have I been vain, proud, selfish or self-seeking?

Have I told lies to excuse myself, to hurt others or to make myself look more important?

Have I stolen anything?

Have I failed to contribute to the support of the Church in proportion to my means?

Have I been disobedient, rude or insolent to those in authority over me?

Have I been harsh, overbearing or sarcastic to those under my authority?

Have I cheated my employers or employees?

Have I misused or damaged the property of others?

Have I set my heart greedily on possessing things?

Have I given scandal or bad example?

Have I been lazy at my work, study or domestic duties?

Have I been jealous of others – of their looks, their popularity, their good work?

Have I encouraged others to do wrong in any way?

For spouses

Have I neglected to foster the warmth of my love and affection for my spouse?

Have I prolonged disagreements through resentment or failing to apologise when I have been in the wrong?

Have I mistreated my spouse verbally, emotionally or physically?

Have I used artificial means of birth control?
Have I been unfaithful to my spouse in any way?

For parents

Have I neglected to teach my children to pray?
Have I neglected the religious education of my children?
Have I failed to bring my children to Sunday Mass?
Have I argued with my spouse in front of my children?
Have I failed to exercise vigilance over what my children read, see on television or on the internet?
Have I been harsh or overbearing to my children?
Have I neglected my children's welfare in any way?

For young people

Have I been disobedient to my parents?
Have I been unhelpful at home?
Have I failed to try to understand my parents and talk with them?
Have I upset the peace of my home for selfish reasons?
Have I lost control when I have been angry?
Have I sulked or been sarcastic instead of asking for help?
Have I failed to work properly at school?
Have I treated teachers or other adults with disrespect?
Have I played unfairly at games or sports?
Have I taken part in fights?

Going to Confession

(*You may take this prayer book with you to Confession*)

Reception

The priest welcomes the penitent warmly. The penitent and priest begin by making the sign of the cross, while saying: ✠ **In the name of the Father, and of the Son, and of the Holy Spirit. Amen.** The priest invites you to trust in God. You may indicate your state of life, and anything else which may help the priest as confessor.

The Word of God

The priest may invite you to reflect on a passage from Holy Scripture, speaking of God's mercy and call to conversion.

Reconciliation

Then you can speak in your own words or you can say: **Bless me Father for I have sinned. My last confession was…ago** (*say roughly how long*) **and these are my sins.** Now tell your sins simply in your own words. When you have finished, let the priest know. You can use these words if you wish: **I am sorry for all these sins and for any that I cannot now remember.**

Listen carefully to the advice of the priest and ask the Holy Spirit to help him to say what is best to help you to grow in the Christian life. You can ask him questions if you want. The priest may propose an Act of Penance, which should serve not only to make up for the past but also to help begin a new life and provide an antidote to weakness. It may take the form of prayer, self-denial, and especially of service to one's neighbour and works of mercy.

Then the priest invites you to say a prayer of sorrow (an Act of Contrition), such as:

O my God, because you are so good, I am very sorry that I have sinned against you, and by the help of your grace I will not sin again.

Wait while the priest says the prayer of "Absolution" (where Christ forgives you all your sins). Make the sign of the cross as the priest says: **I absolve you from your sins in the name of the Father ✠ and of the Son and of the Holy Spirit. Amen.** The priest may say a few final words of encouragement to you as you leave.

After Confession

Take some time in the quiet of the Church to reflect on the grace of the sacrament and to thank God for his mercy and forgiveness. Here is a prayer of thanksgiving:

Father, in your love you have brought me from evil to good and from misery to happiness. Through your blessings give me the courage of perseverance. Amen.

The Way of The Cross

The Way of the Cross is a devotion to the Sacred Passion in which we accompany, in spirit, our Blessed Lord in his sorrowful journey from the house of Pilate to Calvary, and recall, with sorrow and love, all that took place from the time when he was condemned to death to his being laid in the tomb. We meditate devoutly on the Passion and Death of our Lord as we move around the stations in the Church. (Indulgences, page 124).

Often, when made publicly, the following response is said at each station as we genuflect:

V. We adore you, O Christ, and we praise you.
R. Because by your Holy Cross you have redeemed the world.

The following act of contrition may be used at each station:
I love you, Jesus, my love above all things. I repent with my whole heart of having offended you. Never permit me to separate myself from you again. Grant that I may love you always and then do with me what you will.
(*Our Father; Hail Mary; Glory be.*)

I. Jesus is condemned to death

Consider how Jesus, after having been scourged and crowned with thorns, was unjustly condemned by Pilate to die on the Cross.

II. Jesus receives the Cross

Consider how Jesus, in making this journey with the Cross on his shoulders, thought of us, and offered for us to his Father the death he was about to undergo.

III. Jesus falls the first time

Consider the first fall of Jesus under his Cross. His flesh was torn by the scourges, his head was crowned with thorns; he had lost a great quantity of blood. So weakened he could scarcely walk, he yet had to carry this great load upon his shoulders. The soldiers struck him rudely, and he fell several times.

IV. Jesus is met by his Blessed Mother

Consider this meeting of the Son and the Mother, which took place on this journey. Their looks became like so many arrows to wound those hearts which loved each other so tenderly.

V. The Cross is laid upon Simon of Cyrene

Consider how his cruel tormentors, seeing that Jesus was on the point of expiring, and fearing he would die on the way, whereas they wished him to die the shameful death of the Cross, constrained Simon of Cyrene to carry the Cross behind our Lord.

VI. Veronica wipes the face of Jesus

Consider how the holy woman named Veronica, seeing Jesus so ill-used, and bathed in sweat and blood, wiped his face with a towel, on which was left the impression of his holy countenance.

VII. Jesus falls the second time

Consider the second fall of Jesus under the Cross; a fall which renews the pain of all the wounds in his head and members.

VIII. The women of Jerusalem mourn for our Lord

Consider how these women wept with compassion at seeing Jesus in such a pitiable state, streaming with blood, as he walked along. 'Daughters of Jerusalem', said he, 'weep not for me, but for yourselves and for your children'.

IX. Jesus falls the third time

Consider the third fall of Jesus Christ. His weakness was extreme, and the cruelty of his executioners excessive, who tried to hasten his steps when he could scarcely move.

X. Jesus is stripped of his garments

Consider the violence with which Jesus was stripped by the executioners. His inner garments adhered to his torn flesh, and they dragged them off so roughly that the skin came with them. Take pity on your Saviour thus cruelly treated.

XI. Jesus is nailed to the Cross

Consider how Jesus, having been placed upon the Cross, extended his hands, and offered to his Eternal Father the sacrifice of his life for our salvation. Those barbarians fastened him with nails, and then, securing the Cross, allowed him to die with anguish on this infamous gibbet.

XII. Jesus dies on the Cross

Consider how Jesus, being consumed with anguish after three hours' agony on the Cross, abandoned himself to the weight of his body, bowed his head and died.

XIII. Jesus is taken down from the Cross

Consider how, after our Lord had expired, two of his disciples, Joseph and Nicodemus, took him down from the Cross and placed him in the arms of his afflicted Mother, who received him with unutterable tenderness, and pressed him to her bosom.

XIV. Jesus is placed in the sepulchre

Consider how the disciples, accompanied by his holy Mother, carried the body of Jesus to bury it. They closed the tomb, and all came sorrowfully away.

Prayers to Our Lady

The Holy Rosary

The Holy Rosary is composed of twenty 'decades', each comprising the Our Father, ten Hail Marys, and the Glory be, recited in honour of some mystery in the life of Our Lord or his Blessed Mother. We pray to practise the virtue specially taught by that mystery.

I. The Five Joyful Mysteries (*Mondays, Saturdays*)

1. The Annunciation. (*Lk* 1:26-38)
2. The Visitation. (*Lk* 1:39-45)
3. The Nativity. (*Lk* 2:1-7)
4. The Presentation in the Temple. (*Lk* 2: 22-35)
5. The Finding of the Child Jesus in the Temple. (*Lk* 2:41-52)

II. The Five Mysteries of Light (*Thursdays*)

1. The Baptism of the Lord. (*Mt* 3:13-17)
2. The Marriage at Cana. (*Jn* 2:1-12)
3. The Proclamation of the Kingdom and call to conversion. (*Mk* 1:14-15; 2:3-12)
4. The Transfiguration. (*Lk* 9:28-36)
5. The Institution of the Eucharist. (*Mt* 26:26-29)

III. The Five Sorrowful Mysteries (*Tuesdays, Fridays*)
1. The Prayer and Agony in the Garden. (*Mk* 14:32-42)
2. The Scourging at the Pillar. (*Mt* 27:15-26)
3. The Crowning with Thorns. (*Mt* 27:27-31)
4. The Carrying of the Cross. (*Jn* 19:15-17; *Lk* 23:27-32)
5. The Crucifixion and Death. (*Lk* 23:33-38, 44-46)

IV. The Five Glorious Mysteries (*Wednesdays, Sundays*)
1. The Resurrection. (*Mt* 28:1-8)
2. The Ascension of Christ into Heaven. (*Ac* 1:6-11)
3. The Descent of the Holy Spirit. (*Ac* 2:1-12)
4. The Assumption. (1 *Th* 4:13-18)
5. The Coronation of the Blessed Virgin Mary. (*Rv* 12:1; 14:1-5: *Is* 6:1-3)

The Hail Holy Queen

Hail, holy Queen, mother of mercy; hail, our life, our sweetness, and our hope! To you do we cry, poor banished children of Eve; to you do we send up our sighs, mourning and weeping in this vale of tears. Turn then, most gracious advocate, your eyes of mercy towards us; and after this our exile, show unto us the blessed fruit of your womb, Jesus. O clement, O loving, O sweet Virgin Mary.

V. Pray for us, O holy Mother of God.
R. That we may be made worthy of the promises of Christ.

Let us pray: O God, whose only-begotten Son, by his life, death and resurrection, has purchased for us the rewards of eternal life; grant, we beseech you, that meditating on these Mysteries of the most holy Rosary of the Blessed Virgin Mary, we may both imitate what they contain, and obtain what they promise, through the same Christ our Lord. **R. Amen.** (*Indulgences, page* 124)

LITANY OF THE BLESSED VIRGIN MARY

Lord have mercy.
Lord have mercy.
Christ have mercy.
Christ have mercy.
Lord have mercy.
Lord have mercy.
Christ hear us.
Christ graciously hear us.
God the Father of heaven,
have mercy on us. (repeat)
God the Son, Redeemer
of the world,
God the Holy Spirit,
Holy Trinity, one God,
Holy Mary,
pray for us. (repeat)
Holy Mother of God,
Holy Virgin of virgins,
Mother of Christ,
Mother of the Church,
Mother of Mercy,
Mother of divine grace,
Mother of Hope,
Mother most pure,
Mother most chaste,
Mother inviolate,
Mother undefiled,
Mother most lovable,
Mother most admirable,
Mother of good counsel,
Mother of our Creator,
Mother of our Saviour,

Virgin most prudent,
Virgin most venerable,
Virgin most renowned,
Virgin most powerful,
Virgin most merciful,
Virgin most faithful,

Mirror of justice,
Seat of wisdom,
Cause of our joy,
Spiritual vessel,
Vessel of honour,
Singular vessel of devotion,
Mystical rose,
Tower of David,
Tower of ivory,

House of gold,
Ark of the covenant,
Gate of heaven,
Morning Star,
Health of the sick,

Refuge of sinners,
Solace of Migrants,
Comfort of the afflicted,
Help of Christians,

Queen of Angels,
Queen of Patriarchs,
Queen of Prophets,
Queen of Apostles
Queen of Martyrs,
Queen of Confessors,
Queen of Virgins,
Queen of all Saints,
Queen conceived without original sin,
Queen assumed into heaven,
Queen of the most holy Rosary,
Queen of the Family,
Queen of Peace.

Lamb of God, you take away the sins of the world, *spare us, O Lord.*
Lamb of God, you take away the sins of the world, *graciously hear us, O Lord.*
Lamb of God, you take away the sins of the world, *have mercy on us.*

Other Prayers

The Memorare

Remember, O most gracious Virgin Mary, that never was it known that anyone who fled to thy protection, implored thy help, or sought thy intercession was left unaided.

Inspired by this confidence, I fly unto thee, O Virgin of virgins, my mother; to thee do I come, before thee I stand, sinful and sorrowful.

O Mother of the Word Incarnate, despise not my petitions, but in thy mercy hear and answer me. Amen.

The Regina Cæli

V. O Queen of heaven, rejoice! Alleluia.
R. For he whom you did merit to bear, Alleluia,
V. Has risen as he said, Alleluia.
R. Pray for us to God, Alleluia.
V. Rejoice and be glad, O Virgin Mary, Alleluia,
R. For the Lord has risen indeed, Alleluia.

Let us pray: God our Father, you give joy to the world by the Resurrection of your Son, our Lord Jesus Christ. Through the prayers of his Mother, the Virgin Mary, bring us to the happiness of eternal life. We ask this through our Lord Jesus Christ, your Son, who lives and reigns with you and the Holy Spirit, one God, for ever and ever.
R. Amen.

Prayers for Various Needs and Occasions

Act of Faith

My God, I believe in you and all that your Church teaches, because you have said it, and your word is true.

Act of Hope

My God, I hope in you, for grace and for glory, because of your promises, your mercy and your power.

Act of Charity

My God, because you are so good, I love you with all my heart, and for your sake, I love my neighbour as myself.

Commendation

Jesus, Mary and Joseph, I give you my heart and my soul.
Jesus, Mary and Joseph, assist me in my last agony.
Jesus, Mary and Joseph, may I breathe forth my soul in peace with you.

Act of Resignation

O Lord, my God, whatever manner of death is pleasing to you, with all its anguish, pains and sorrows, I now accept from your hand with a resigned and willing spirit. (*Indulgences, page* 124)

For the Faithful Departed

Out of the depths I cry to you, O Lord,
Lord hear my voice!
O let your ears be attentive
to the voice of my pleading.

> If you, O Lord, should mark our guilt,
> Lord, who would survive?
> But with you is found forgiveness:
> for this we revere you.

My soul is waiting for the Lord,
I count on his word.
My soul is longing for the Lord
more than watchmen for daybreak.
Let the watchman count on daybreak
and Israel on the Lord.

> Because with the Lord there is mercy
> and fullness of redemption;
> Israel indeed he will redeem
> from all its iniquity.

(*Psalm 130*)

V. Eternal rest grant to them, O Lord.

R. And let perpetual light shine upon them.

V. May they rest in peace.

R. Amen.

Let us pray:
O God, the Creator and Redeemer of all the faithful, grant to the souls of your servants departed the remission of all their sins, that through our pious supplication they may obtain that pardon which they have always desired; who live and reign for ever and ever. **R. Amen.**

For help

May the divine assistance remain always with us ✠ and may the souls of the faithful departed, through the mercy of God, rest in peace. Amen.

Prayer of Saint Ignatius

Teach us, good Lord, to serve you as you deserve; to give and not to count the cost; to fight and not to heed the wounds; to toil and not to seek for rest; to labour and not to ask for any reward, save that of knowing that we do your will. Amen.

Prayer of Saint Richard of Chichester

Thanks be to you, my Lord, Jesus Christ, for all the benefits which you have given me, for all the pains and insults which you have borne for me. O most merciful Redeemer, friend and brother, may I know you more clearly, love you more dearly, and follow you more nearly, day by day. Amen.

Prayer to my guardian angel

O angel of God, my guardian dear
to whom God's love commits me here.
Ever this day/night be at my side
to light, to guard, to rule and guide.
Amen.

Prayer to Saint Michael

St Michael, the Archangel, defend us in the day of battle; be our safeguard against the wickedness and snares of the devil. May God rebuke him, we humbly pray and do you, O Prince of the heavenly host, by the power of God, cast into hell Satan and all the other evil spirits who prowl through the world seeking the ruin of souls. Amen.

Prayer for Life

O Mary, bright dawn of the new world, Mother of the living, to you do we entrust the cause of life.

Look down, O Mother, on the vast numbers of babies not allowed to be born, of the poor whose lives are made difficult, of men and women who are victims of brutal violence, of the elderly and the sick killed by indifference or out of misguided mercy.

Grant that all who believe in your Son may proclaim the Gospel of life with honesty and love to the people of our time.

Obtain for them the grace to accept that Gospel as a gift ever new, the joy of celebrating it with gratitude throughout their lives and the courage to bear witness to it resolutely, in order to build, together with all people of good will, the civilization of truth and love, to the praise and glory of God, the Creator and lover of life. (*Pope John Paul II*)

In Temptation

Lord, save me, or I perish. Keep me close to you by your grace, or I shall sin and fall away from you. Jesus, help me; Mary, help me; my holy Angel, watch over me.

In Trouble

In all things may the most holy, the most just, and the most lovable will of God be done, praised, and exalted above all for ever. Your will be done, O Lord, your will be done. The Lord has given, the Lord has taken away; blessed be the name of the Lord.

In Sickness and Pain

Lord, your will be done; I take this for my sins. I offer up to you my sufferings, together with all that my Saviour has suffered for me; and I beg you, through his sufferings, to have mercy on me. Free me from this illness and pain if you will, and if it be for my good. You love me too much to let me suffer unless it be for my good. Therefore,

O Lord, I trust myself to you; do with me as you please. In sickness and in health, I wish to love you always.

Prayer for Chastity

O my God, teach me to love others with the purity of your holy Mother. Give me the grace to resist firmly every temptation to impure thoughts, words or actions. Teach me always to love with generosity and goodness, to respect myself and others in the way I act and to reverence the way that you have given us for the creation of new life.

In Thanksgiving

My God, from my heart I thank you for the many blessings you have given to me. I thank you for having created and baptised me, and for having placed me in your holy Catholic Church; and for having given me so many graces and mercies through the merits of Jesus Christ. And I thank you, dear Jesus, for having become a little child for my sake, to teach me to be holy and humble like you; and for having died upon the Cross that I might have pardon for my sins and get to heaven. Also I thank you for all your other mercies, most of all for those you have given me today.

Prayer for the Pope

O almighty and eternal God, have mercy on your servant our Holy Father, the Pope, and direct him according to your clemency into the way of everlasting salvation; that he may desire by your grace those things that are agreeable to you, and perform them with all his strength. Through Christ our Lord. Amen.

Prayer for Priests

Father, you have appointed your Son Jesus Christ eternal High Priest. Guide those he has chosen to be ministers of word and sacrament and help them to be faithful in fulfilling the ministry they have received. Grant this through our Lord Jesus Christ, your Son, who lives and reigns with you and the Holy Spirit, one God, for ever and ever. Amen.

Prayer for Vocations

Lord Jesus Christ, Shepherd of souls, who called the Apostles to be fishers of men, raise up new apostles in your holy Church. Teach them that to serve you is to reign: to possess you is to possess all things. Kindle in the young hearts of our sons and daughters the fire of zeal for souls. Make them eager to spread your Kingdom on earth. Grant them courage to follow you, who are the Way, the Truth and the Life; who live and reign for ever and ever. Amen.

Mary, Queen of the Clergy, pray for us. Help our students who are preparing for the priesthood.

Prayer for Others

O Jesus, have mercy on your holy Church; take care of her.

O Jesus, have pity on poor sinners, and save them from hell.

O Jesus, bless my father, my mother, my brothers and sisters, and all I ought to pray for, as your Heart knows how to bless them.

O Jesus, have pity on the poor souls in purgatory and give them eternal rest.

Prayer for Christian Unity

Look mercifully, Lord, on your people, and pour out on us the gifts of your Holy Spirit. Grant that we may constantly grow in love of the truth, and seek the perfect unity of Christians in our prayers and our deeds. Through Christ our Lord. Amen.

Prayer for Peace

O God, from whom are holy desires, right counsels and just deeds, give to your servants that peace which the world cannot give; that we may serve you with our whole hearts, and live quiet lives under your protection, free from the fear of our enemies. Through Christ our Lord. Amen.

Anima Christi

Soul of Christ, sanctify me.
Body of Christ, save me.
Blood of Christ, inebriate me.
Water from the side of Christ, wash me.
Passion of Christ, strengthen me.
O good Jesus, hear me.
Within thy wounds hide me.
Suffer me not to be separated from thee.
From the malicious enemy defend me.
In the hour of my death call me,
And bid me to come to thee.
That with thy saints I may praise thee,
For all eternity. Amen.

Prayer before a Crucifix

Behold, O kind and most sweet Jesus, I cast myself on my knees in your sight, and with the most fervent desire of my soul, I pray and beseech you that you would impress upon my heart lively sentiments of faith, hope, and charity, with a true repentance for my sins, and a firm desire of amendment, while with deep affection and grief of soul I ponder within myself and mentally contemplate your five most precious wounds; having before my eyes that which David spoke in prophecy of you, O good Jesus: 'They pierced my hands and my feet; they have numbered all my bones'. (*Indulgences, page* 124)

Grace before meals

☧ Bless us, O Lord, and these your gifts which we are about to receive from your bounty. Through Christ our Lord. Amen.

Grace after meals

☧ We give you thanks, almighty God, for all your benefits, who live and reign, world without end. Amen.

☧ May the souls of the faithful departed, through the mercy of God, rest in peace. Amen.

A Night Prayer (*Lk* 2:29-32)

Antiphon:
Save us Lord, while we are awake;
protect us while we sleep;
that we may keep watch with Christ
and rest with him in peace.

At last, all-powerful Master,
you give leave to your servant
to go in peace, according to your promise.
   For my eyes have seen your salvation
   which you have prepared for all nations,
   the light to enlighten the gentiles
   and give glory to Israel, your people.
     Glory be to the Father…
Antiphon: Save us Lord…

The Divine Mercy

The devotion consists in the adoration of Mercy, the heart of which is trust, meaning to assume an attitude conforming to Jesus' will. Trustful believers are assured many graces in this world and eternal happiness in the next. The Novena of the Divine Mercy (which includes the Chaplet, and other prayers) begins on Good Friday and ends on Divine Mercy Sunday.

The Chaplet

Prayed on ordinary rosary beads, in the following order: The Our Father, Hail Mary, Apostle's Creed. *On the large bead before each decade:*

Eternal Father, I offer you the Body and Blood, Soul and Divinity of Your dearly beloved Son, Our Lord Jesus Christ, in atonement for our sins and those of the world.

Once on each of the ten small beads:

For the sake of His sorrowful Passion, have mercy on us and on the whole world.

Concluding doxology: after five decades repeat three times:

Holy God, Holy Mighty One, Holy Immortal One, have mercy on us and the whole world.

O Blood and Water

O Blood and Water, which gushed forth from the heart of Jesus as a Fount of Mercy for us, I trust in you.

The Litany of the Divine Mercy

Divine Mercy, gushing forth from the bosom of the Father,
I Trust in You. (Repeat this after each line)
Divine Mercy, greatest attribute of God,
Divine Mercy, incomprehensible mystery,
Divine Mercy, fountain gushing forth from the mystery of
    the Most Blessed Trinity,
Divine Mercy, unfathomed by any intellect, human or angelic,
Divine Mercy, from which wells forth all life and happiness,
Divine Mercy, better than the heavens,
Divine Mercy, source of miracles and wonders,
Divine Mercy, encompassing the whole universe,
Divine Mercy, descending to earth in the Person of
    the Incarnate Word,
Divine Mercy, which flowed out from the open wound of
    the Heart of Jesus,
Divine Mercy, enclosed in the Heart of Jesus for us,
    and especially for sinners,
Divine Mercy, unfathomed in the institution
    of the Sacred Heart,
Divine Mercy, in the founding of Holy Church,
Divine Mercy, in the Sacrament of Holy Baptism,
Divine Mercy, in our justification through Jesus Christ,

Divine Mercy, accompanying us through our whole life,
Divine Mercy, embracing us especially at the hour of death,
Divine Mercy, endowing us with immortal life,
Divine Mercy, accompanying us every moment of our life,
Divine Mercy, shielding us from the fire of hell,
Divine Mercy, in the conversion of hardened sinners,
Divine Mercy, astonishment for Angels,
    incomprehensible to Saints,
Divine Mercy, unfathomed in all the mysteries of God,
Divine Mercy, lifting us out of every misery,
Divine Mercy, source of our happiness and joy,
Divine Mercy, in calling us forth from nothingness
    to existence,
Divine Mercy, embracing all the works of His hands,
Divine Mercy, crown of all of God's handiwork,
Divine Mercy, in which we are all immersed,
Divine Mercy, sweet relief for anguished hearts,
Divine Mercy, only hope of despairing souls,
Divine Mercy, repose of hearts, peace amidst fear,
Divine Mercy, delight and ecstacy of holy souls,
Divine Mercy, inspiring hope against all hope.

Let us pray: Eternal God, in whom mercy is endless and the treasury of compassion inexhaustible, look kindly upon us and increase Your mercy in us, that in difficult moments we might not despair nor become despondent, but with great confidence submit ourselves to Your holy will, which is Love and Mercy itself. Amen.

THE EUCHARIST
The Order of Mass

Introductory Rites

The faithful dispose themselves properly to celebrate the Eucharist.

Before Mass begins, the people gather in a spirit of recollection, preparing for their participation in the Mass. All stand during the entrance procession.

Sign of the Cross

After the Entrance Chant, the Priest and the faithful sign themselves with the Sign of the Cross:

Priest: In the name of the Father, and of the Son, and of the Holy Spirit.

Response: Amen.

Greeting

The Priest greets the people, with one of the following:

1. Pr. The grace of our Lord Jesus Christ,
and the love of God,
and the communion of the Holy Spirit
be with you all.

2. Pr. Grace to you and peace from God our Father
and the Lord Jesus Christ.

3. Pr. The Lord be with you.

The people reply:
R. **And with your spirit.**
The Priest, or a Deacon, or another minister, may very briefly introduce the faithful to the Mass of the day.

Penitential Act

There are three forms of the Penitential Act which may be chosen from as appropriate.
Pr. Brethren (brothers and sisters),
   let us acknowledge our sins,
and so prepare ourselves to celebrate the sacred
   mysteries.
A brief pause for silence follows.
Then one of the following forms is used:

---

1. I confess to almighty God
and to you, my brothers and sisters,
that I have greatly sinned,
in my thoughts and in my words,
in what I have done and in what I have failed to do,
(*and, striking their breast, they say*:)
through my fault, through my fault,
through my most grievous fault;
therefore I ask blessed Mary ever-Virgin,
all the Angels and Saints,
and you, my brothers and sisters,
to pray for me to the Lord our God.

The Order of Mass

2. Pr. Have mercy on us, O Lord.
R. For we have sinned against you.
Pr. Show us, O Lord, your mercy.
R. And grant us your salvation.

Invocations naming the gracious works of the Lord may be made, as in the example below:

3. Pr. You were sent to heal the contrite of heart:
Lord, have mercy.   *Or*:   Kyrie, eleison.
R. Lord, have mercy.   *Or*:   **Kyrie, eleison.**
Pr. You came to call sinners:
Christ, have mercy.   *Or*:   Christe, eleison.
R. Christ, have mercy.   *Or*:   **Christe, eleison.**
Pr. You are seated at the right hand of the Father to intercede for us:
Lord, have mercy.   *Or*:   Kyrie, eleison.
R. Lord, have mercy.   *Or*:   **Kyrie, eleison.**

The absolution by the Priest follows:
Pr. May almighty God have mercy on us,
forgive us our sins,
and bring us to everlasting life.
R. Amen.

The Kyrie, eleison (Lord, have mercy) *invocations follow, unless they have just occurred.*

Pr. Lord, have mercy.   **R. Lord, have mercy.**
Pr. Christ, have mercy.   **R. Christ, have mercy.**
Pr. Lord, have mercy.   **R. Lord, have mercy.**
Or:
Pr. Kyrie, eleison.   **R. Kyrie, eleison.**
Pr. Christe, eleison.   **R. Christe, eleison.**
Pr. Kyrie, eleison.   **R. Kyrie, eleison.**

The Gloria

On Sundays (outside of Advent and Lent), Solemnities and Feast Days, this hymn is either sung or said:

Glory to God in the highest,
and on earth peace to people of good will.

We praise you,
we bless you,
we adore you,
we glorify you,
we give you thanks for your great glory,
Lord God, heavenly King,
O God, almighty Father.

Lord Jesus Christ, Only Begotten Son,
Lord God, Lamb of God, Son of the Father,
you take away the sins of the world, have mercy on us;
you take away the sins of the world, receive our prayer;
you are seated at the right hand of the Father,
   have mercy on us.

The Order of Mass

**For you alone are the Holy One,
you alone are the Lord,
you alone are the Most High,
Jesus Christ,
with the Holy Spirit,
in the glory of God the Father.
Amen.**

Glória in excélsis Deo
et in terra pax homínibus bonæ voluntátis.
Laudámus te,
benedícimus te,
adorámus te,
glorificámus te,
grátias ágimus tibi propter magnam glóriam tuam.
Dómine Deus, Rex cæléstis,
Deus Pater omnípotens.
Dómine Fili unigénite, Jesu Christe,
Dómine Deus, Agnus Dei, Fílius Patris,
qui tollis peccáta mundi, miserére nobis;
qui tollis peccáta mundi, súscipe deprecatiónem nostram.
Qui sedes ad déxteram Patris, miserére nobis.
Quóniam tu solus Sanctus, tu solus Dóminus, tu solus
  Altissimus,
Jesu Christe, cum Sancto Spíritu: in glória Dei Patris.
Amen.

When this hymn is concluded, the Priest, says:
Pr. Let us pray.
And all pray in silence. Then the Priest says the Collect prayer, which ends:
R. Amen.

THE LITURGY OF THE WORD

By hearing the word proclaimed in worship, the faithful again enter into a dialogue with God.

First Reading

The reader goes to the ambo and proclaims the First Reading, while all sit and listen. The reader ends:
The word of the Lord.
R. Thanks be to God.
It is appropriate to have a brief time of quiet between readings as those present take the word of God to heart.

Psalm

The psalmist or cantor sings or says the Psalm, with the people making the response.

Second Reading

On Sundays and certain other days there is a second reading. It concludes with the same response as above.

Gospel

The assembly stands for the Gospel Acclamation. Except during Lent the Acclamation is:

R. Alleluia

During Lent the following forms are used:

R. Praise to you, O Christ, King of eternal glory! *Or*:

R. Praise and honour to you, Lord Jesus! *Or*:

R. Glory and praise to you, O Christ! *Or*:

R. Glory to you, O Christ, you are the Word of God!

At the ambo the Deacon, or the Priest says:

Pr. The Lord be with you.

R. And with your spirit.

Pr. A reading from the holy Gospel according to N.

He makes the Sign of the Cross on the book and, together with the people, on his forehead, lips, and breast.

R. Glory to you, O Lord.

At the end of the Gospel:

Pr. The Gospel of the Lord.

R. Praise to you, Lord Jesus Christ.

After the Gospel all sit to listen to the homily.

The Homily

Then follows the Homily, which is preached by a Priest or Deacon on all Sundays and Holydays of Obligation. After a brief silence all stand.

The Creed

On Sundays and Solemnities, the Profession of Faith will follow. The Apostles' Creed may be used.

The Niceno-Constantinopolitan Creed

I believe in one God,
the Father almighty,
maker of heaven and earth,
of all things visible and invisible.

I believe in one Lord Jesus Christ,
the Only Begotten Son of God,
born of the Father before all ages.
God from God, Light from Light,
true God from true God,
begotten, not made, consubstantial with the Father;
through him all things were made.
For us men and for our salvation
he came down from heaven, *(all bow)*
and by the Holy Spirit was incarnate of the Virgin Mary,
and became man.

For our sake he was crucified under Pontius Pilate,
he suffered death and was buried,
and rose again on the third day
in accordance with the Scriptures.
He ascended into heaven
and is seated at the right hand of the Father.
He will come again in glory
to judge the living and the dead
and his kingdom will have no end.

**I believe in the Holy Spirit, the Lord, the giver of life,
who proceeds from the Father and the Son,
who with the Father and the Son is adored and glorified,
who has spoken through the prophets.**

**I believe in one, holy, catholic and apostolic Church.
I confess one Baptism for the forgiveness of sins
and I look forward to the resurrection of the dead
and the life of the world to come. Amen.**

Credo in unum Deum,
Patrem omnipoténtem, factórem cæli et terræ,
visibílium ómnium et invisibílium.
Et in unum Dóminum Jesum Christum,
Fílium Dei unigénitum,
et ex Patre natum ante ómnia sǽcula.
Deum de Deo, lumen de lúmine, Deum verum de Deo vero,
génitum, non factum, consubstantiálem Patri:
per quem ómnia facta sunt.
Qui propter nos hómines et propter nostram salútem
descéndit de cælis. *(all bow)*
Et incarnátus est de Spiritu Sancto
ex María Vírgine, et homo factus est.
Crucifíxus étiam pro nobis sub Póntio Piláto;
passus et sepúltus est,
et resurréxit tértia die, secúndum Scriptúras,
et ascéndit in cælum, sedet ad déxteram Patris.

Et íterum ventúrus est cum glória, judicáre vivos et
    mórtuos,
cujus regni non erit finis.
Et in Spiritum Sanctum, Dóminum et vivificántem:
qui ex Patre Filióque procédit.
Qui cum Patre et Fílio simul adorátur et conglorificátur:
qui locútus est per prophétas.
Et unam, sanctam, cathólicam et apostólicam Ecclésiam.
Confíteor unum baptísma in remissiónem peccatórum.
Et exspécto resurrectiónem mortuórum,
et vitam ventúri sæculi. Amen.

The Apostles' Creed

**I believe in God,
the Father almighty,
Creator of heaven and earth,
and in Jesus Christ, his only Son, our Lord,** *(all bow)*
**who was conceived by the Holy Spirit,
born of the Virgin Mary,
suffered under Pontius Pilate,
was crucified, died and was buried;
he descended into hell;
on the third day he rose again from the dead;
he ascended into heaven,
and is seated at the right hand of God the Father
    almighty;**

from there he will come to judge the living and the dead.

I believe in the Holy Spirit,
the holy catholic Church,
the communion of saints,
the forgiveness of sins,
the resurrection of the body,
and life everlasting. Amen.

Credo in Deum,
Patrem omnipoténtem, Creatórem cæli et terræ.
Et in Iesum Christum, Fílium eius únicum, Dóminum nostrum: (*all bow*)
qui concéptus est de Spíritu Sancto,
natus ex María Vírgine,
passus sub Póntio Piláto,
crucifíxus, mórtuus, et sepúltus;
descéndit ad inferos;
tértia die resurréxit a mórtuis;
ascéndit ad cælos;
sedet ad déxteram Dei Patris omnipoténtis;
inde ventúrus est iudicáre vivos et mórtuos.
Credo in Spíritum Sanctum,
sanctam Ecclésiam Cathólicam,
Sanctórum communiónem,
remissiónem peccatórum,
carnis resurrectiónem,
vitam ætérnam. Amen.

The Prayer of the Faithful (Bidding Prayers)

Intentions will normally be for the Church; for the world; for those in particular need; and for the local community. After each there is time for silent prayer, followed by the next intention, or concluded with a sung phrase such as **Christ, hear us**, *or* **Christ graciously hear us**, *or by a responsory such as*:

Let us pray to the Lord.
R. Grant this, almighty God. *Or:*
R. Lord, have mercy. *Or:*
R. Kyrie, eleison.
The Priest concludes the Prayer with a collect.

THE LITURGY OF THE EUCHARIST

For Catholics, the Eucharist is the source and summit of the whole Christian Life.

After the Liturgy of the Word, the people sit and the Offertory Chant begins. The faithful express their participation by making an offering, bringing forward bread and wine for the celebration of the Eucharist.

Preparatory Prayers

Standing at the altar, the Priest takes the paten with the bread and holds it slightly raised above the altar with both hands, saying:
Pr. Blessed are you, Lord God of all creation,
for through your goodness we have received

the bread we offer you:
fruit of the earth and work of human hands,
it will become for us the bread of life.

R. Blessed be God for ever.

The Priest then takes the chalice and holds it slightly raised above the altar with both hands, saying:

Pr. Blessed are you, Lord God of all creation,
for through your goodness we have received
the wine we offer you:
fruit of the vine and work of human hands,
it will become our spiritual drink.

R. Blessed be God for ever.

The Priest completes additional personal preparatory rites, and the people rise as he says:

Pr. Pray, brethren (brothers and sisters),
that my sacrifice and yours
may be acceptable to God,
the almighty Father.

**R. May the Lord accept the sacrifice at your hands
for the praise and glory of his name,
for our good
and the good of all his holy Church.**

The Prayer over the Offerings

The Priest says the Prayer over the Offerings, at the end of which the people acclaim: **R. Amen.**

The Eucharistic Prayer

Extending his hands, the Priest says:

Pr. The Lord be with you.

R. And with your spirit.

Pr. Lift up your hearts.

R. We lift them up to the Lord.

Pr. Let us give thanks to the Lord our God.

R. It is right and just.

The Priest continues with the Preface appropriate to the Season or Feast at the end of which all sing or say:

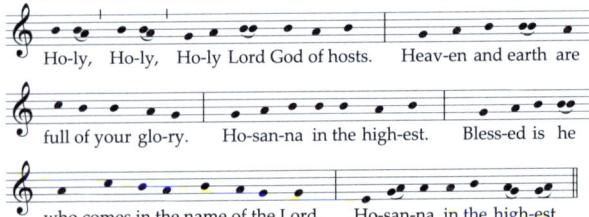

Holy, Holy, Holy Lord God of hosts.
Heaven and earth are full of your glory.
Hosanna in the highest.
Blessed is he who comes in the name of the Lord.
Hosanna in the highest.

After the Sanctus the congregation kneels for the remainder of the Eucharistic Prayer. (Texts for the four principal Eucharistic Prayers follow: Eucharistic Prayer I at p. 71, II at p. 77, III at p. 81, IV at p. 85.)

The Order of Mass

Eucharistic Prayer I
(The Roman Canon)

Pr. To you, therefore, most merciful Father,
we make humble prayer and petition
through Jesus Christ, your Son, our Lord:
that you accept
and bless ✠ these gifts, these offerings,
these holy and unblemished sacrifices,
which we offer you firstly
for your holy catholic Church.
Be pleased to grant her peace,
to guard, unite and govern her
throughout the whole world,
together with your servant N. our Pope and N. our Bishop,[*]
and all those who, holding to the truth,
hand on the catholic and apostolic faith.

Remember, Lord, your servants N. and N.
and all gathered here,
whose faith and devotion are known to you.
For them, we offer you this sacrifice of praise
or they offer it for themselves
and all who are dear to them:
for the redemption of their souls,
in hope of health and well-being,
and paying their homage to you,
the eternal God, living and true.

---

[*] Mention may be made here of the Coadjutor Bishop, or Auxiliary Bishops.

In communion with those whose memory we venerate,
especially the glorious ever-Virgin Mary,
Mother of our God and Lord, Jesus Christ,
and blessed Joseph, her Spouse,
your blessed Apostles and Martyrs,
Peter and Paul, Andrew,
(James, John,
Thomas, James, Philip,
Bartholomew, Matthew,
Simon and Jude;
Linus, Cletus, Clement, Sixtus,
Cornelius, Cyprian,
Lawrence, Chrysogonus,
John and Paul,
Cosmas and Damian)
and all your Saints;
we ask that through their merits and prayers,
in all things we may be defended
by your protecting help.
(Through Christ our Lord. Amen.)

Therefore, Lord, we pray:
graciously accept this oblation of our service,
that of your whole family;
order our days in your peace,
and command that we be delivered from eternal damnation
and counted among the flock of those you have chosen.
(Through Christ our Lord. Amen.)

Be pleased, O God, we pray,
to bless, acknowledge,
and approve this offering in every respect;
make it spiritual and acceptable,
so that it may become for us
the Body and Blood of your most beloved Son,
our Lord Jesus Christ.

On the day before he was to suffer,
he took bread in his holy and venerable hands,
and with eyes raised to heaven
to you, O God, his almighty Father,
giving you thanks, he said the blessing,
broke the bread
and gave it to his disciples, saying:

'Take this, all of you, and eat of it,
for this is my Body,
which will be given up for you.'

In a similar way, when supper was ended,
he took this precious chalice
in his holy and venerable hands,
and once more giving you thanks, he said the blessing
and gave the chalice to his disciples, saying:

'Take this, all of you, and drink from it,
for this is the chalice of my Blood,
the Blood of the new and eternal covenant,
which will be poured out for you and for many
for the forgiveness of sins.
Do this in memory of me.'

Pr. The mystery of faith.

The people continue, acclaiming one of the following:

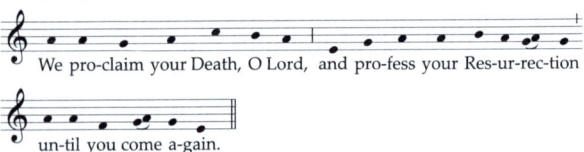

**1. We proclaim your Death, O Lord,
and profess your Resurrection
until you come again.**

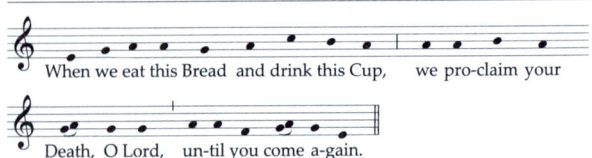

**2. When we eat this Bread and drink this Cup,
we proclaim your Death, O Lord,
until you come again.**

**3. Save us, Saviour of the world,
for by your Cross and Resurrection
you have set us free.**

Pr. Therefore, O Lord,
as we celebrate the memorial of the blessed Passion,
the Resurrection from the dead,
and the glorious Ascension into heaven
of Christ, your Son, our Lord,
we, your servants and your holy people,
offer to your glorious majesty
from the gifts that you have given us,
this pure victim,
this holy victim,
this spotless victim,
the holy Bread of eternal life
and the Chalice of everlasting salvation.

    Be pleased to look upon these offerings
with a serene and kindly countenance,
and to accept them,
as once you were pleased to accept
the gifts of your servant Abel the just,
the sacrifice of Abraham, our father in faith,
and the offering of your high priest Melchizedek,
a holy sacrifice, a spotless victim.

    In humble prayer we ask you, almighty God:
command that these gifts be borne
by the hands of your holy Angel
to your altar on high
in the sight of your divine majesty,
so that all of us, who through this participation at the altar

receive the most holy Body and Blood of your Son,
may be filled with every grace and heavenly blessing.
(Through Christ our Lord. Amen.)

    Remember also, Lord, your servants N. and N.,
who have gone before us with the sign of faith
and rest in the sleep of peace.
Grant them, O Lord, we pray,
and all who sleep in Christ,
a place of refreshment, light and peace.
(Through Christ our Lord. Amen.)
To us, also, your servants, who, though sinners,
hope in your abundant mercies,
graciously grant some share
and fellowship with your holy Apostles and Martyrs:
with John the Baptist, Stephen,
Matthias, Barnabas,
(Ignatius, Alexander,
Marcellinus, Peter,
Felicity, Perpetua,
Agatha, Lucy,
Agnes, Cecilia, Anastasia)
and all your Saints;
admit us, we beseech you,
into their company,
not weighing our merits,
but granting us your pardon,
through Christ our Lord.

The Order of Mass

Through whom
you continue to make all these good things, O Lord;
you sanctify them, fill them with life,
bless them, and bestow them upon us.

The Priest takes the chalice and the paten with the host:
Pr. Through him, and with him, and in him,
O God, almighty Father,
in the unity of the Holy Spirit,
all glory and honour is yours,
for ever and ever.
R. Amen.
Then follows the Communion Rite, p. 90.

Eucharistic Prayer II

Pr. The Lord be with you.
R. And with your spirit.
Pr. Lift up your hearts.
R. We lift them up to the Lord.
Pr. Let us give thanks to the Lord our God.
R. It is right and just.
Pr. It is truly right and just, our duty and our salvation,
always and everywhere to give you thanks, Father most holy,
through your beloved Son, Jesus Christ,
your Word through whom you made all things,
whom you sent as our Saviour and Redeemer,
incarnate by the Holy Spirit and born of the Virgin.

Fulfilling your will and gaining for you a holy people,

he stretched out his hands as he endured his Passion,
so as to break the bonds of death and manifest the
   resurrection.
   And so, with the Angels and all the Saints
we declare your glory,
as with one voice we acclaim:
The people sing or say aloud the Sanctus as on page 63.
Pr. You are indeed Holy, O Lord,
the fount of all holiness.
Make holy, therefore, these gifts, we pray,
by sending down your Spirit upon them like the dewfall,
so that they may become for us
the Body and ✠ Blood of our Lord Jesus Christ.
   At the time he was betrayed
and entered willingly into his Passion,
he took bread and, giving thanks, broke it,
and gave it to his disciples, saying:

> 'TAKE THIS, ALL OF YOU, AND EAT OF IT,
> FOR THIS IS MY BODY,
> WHICH WILL BE GIVEN UP FOR YOU.'

In a similar way, when supper was ended,
he took the chalice
and, once more giving thanks,
he gave it to his disciples, saying:

> 'TAKE THIS, ALL OF YOU, AND DRINK FROM IT,
> FOR THIS IS THE CHALICE OF MY BLOOD,
> THE BLOOD OF THE NEW AND ETERNAL COVENANT,

WHICH WILL BE POURED OUT FOR YOU AND FOR MANY
FOR THE FORGIVENESS OF SINS.
DO THIS IN MEMORY OF ME.'

Pr. The mystery of faith.
The people continue with one of the acclamations on page 74.

Pr. Therefore, as we celebrate
the memorial of his Death and Resurrection,
we offer you, Lord,
the Bread of life and the Chalice of salvation,
giving thanks that you have held us worthy
to be in your presence and minister to you.
Humbly we pray
that, partaking of the Body and Blood of Christ,
we may be gathered into one by the Holy Spirit.
    Remember, Lord, your Church,
spread throughout the world,
and bring her to the fullness of charity,
together with **N.** our Pope and **N.** our Bishop*
and all the clergy.

In Masses for the Dead, the following may be added:
Remember your servant **N.**,
whom you have called (today)
from this world to yourself.

---

* Mention may be made here of the Coadjutor Bishop, or Auxiliary Bishops.

Grant that he (she) who was united with your Son
   in a death like his,
may also be one with him in his Resurrection.

Remember also our brothers and sisters
who have fallen asleep in the hope of the resurrection,
and all who have died in your mercy:
welcome them into the light of your face.
Have mercy on us all, we pray,
that with the Blessed Virgin Mary, Mother of God,
with blessed Joseph, her Spouse,
with the blessed Apostles,
and all the Saints who have pleased you throughout the ages,
we may merit to be coheirs to eternal life,
and may praise and glorify you
through your Son, Jesus Christ.

The Priest takes the chalice and the paten with the host:
Through him, and with him, and in him,
O God, almighty Father,
in the unity of the Holy Spirit,
all glory and honour is yours,
for ever and ever.
R. Amen.
Then follows the Communion Rite, p. 90.

Eucharistic Prayer III

Pr. You are indeed Holy, O Lord,
and all you have created
rightly gives you praise,
for through your Son our Lord Jesus Christ,
by the power and working of the Holy Spirit,
you give life to all things and make them holy,
and you never cease to gather a people to yourself,
so that from the rising of the sun to its setting
a pure sacrifice may be offered to your name.

Therefore, O Lord, we humbly implore you:
by the same Spirit graciously make holy
these gifts we have brought to you for consecration,
that they may become the Body and ✠ Blood
of your Son our Lord Jesus Christ,
at whose command we celebrate these mysteries.

For on the night he was betrayed
he himself took bread,
and, giving you thanks, he said the blessing,
broke the bread and gave it to his disciples, saying:

> 'TAKE THIS, ALL OF YOU,
> AND EAT OF IT, FOR THIS IS MY BODY,
> WHICH WILL BE GIVEN UP FOR YOU.'

In a similar way, when supper was ended,
he took the chalice,
and, giving you thanks, he said the blessing,
and gave the chalice to his disciples, saying:

'Take this, all of you, and drink from it,
for this is the chalice of my Blood
the Blood of the new and eternal covenant,
which will be poured out for you and for many
for the forgiveness of sins.
Do this in memory of me.'

Pr. The mystery of faith.

The people continue with one of the acclamations on page 74.

Pr. Therefore, O Lord, as we celebrate the memorial
of the saving Passion of your Son,
his wondrous Resurrection
and Ascension into heaven,
and as we look forward to his second coming,
we offer you in thanksgiving
this holy and living sacrifice.

Look, we pray, upon the oblation of your Church
and, recognizing the sacrificial Victim by whose death
you willed to reconcile us to yourself,
grant that we, who are nourished
by the Body and Blood of your Son
and filled with his Holy Spirit,
may become one body, one spirit in Christ.

May he make of us
an eternal offering to you,
so that we may obtain an inheritance with your elect,
especially with the most Blessed Virgin Mary,
    Mother of God,

with blessed Joseph, her Spouse,
with your blessed Apostles and glorious Martyrs
(with Saint N.: *the Saint of the day or Patron Saint*)
and with all the Saints,
on whose constant intercession in your presence
we rely for unfailing help.

    May this Sacrifice of our reconciliation,
we pray, O Lord,
advance the peace and salvation of all the world.
Be pleased to confirm in faith and charity
your pilgrim Church on earth,
with your servant N. our Pope and N. our Bishop[*],
the Order of Bishops, all the clergy,
and the entire people you have gained for your own.

    Listen graciously to the prayers of this family,
whom you have summoned before you:
in your compassion, O merciful Father,
gather to yourself all your children
scattered throughout the world.

    † To our departed brothers and sisters
and to all who were pleasing to you
at their passing from this life,
give kind admittance to your kingdom.
There we hope to enjoy for ever the fullness of your glory
through Christ our Lord,
through whom you bestow on the world all that is good.†

---

[*] Mention may be made here of the Coadjutor Bishop, or Auxiliary Bishops.

The Priest takes the chalice and the paten with the host:
Through him, and with him, and in him,
O God, almighty Father,
in the unity of the Holy Spirit,
all glory and honour is yours,
for ever and ever.
R. Amen.
Then follows the Communion Rite, p. 90.

When this Eucharistic Prayer is used in Masses for the Dead, the following may be said:
† Remember your servant N.
whom you have called (today)
from this world to yourself.
Grant that he (she) who was united with your Son
   in a death like his,
may also be one with him in his Resurrection,
when from the earth
he will raise up in the flesh those who have died,
and transform our lowly body
after the pattern of his own glorious body.
To our departed brothers and sisters, too,
and to all who were pleasing to you
at their passing from this life,
give kind admittance to your kingdom.
There we hope to enjoy for ever the fullness of your glory,
when you will wipe away every tear from our eyes.

For seeing you, our God, as you are,
we shall be like you for all the ages
and praise you without end, (*He joins his hands.*)
through Christ our Lord,
through whom you bestow on the world all that is good.†

Eucharistic Prayer IV

Pr. The Lord be with you.
R. And with your spirit.
Pr. Lift up your hearts.
R. We lift them up to the Lord.
Pr. Let us give thanks to the Lord our God.
R. It is right and just.
Pr. It is truly right to give you thanks,
truly just to give you glory, Father most holy,
for you are the one God living and true,
existing before all ages and abiding for all eternity,
dwelling in unapproachable light;
yet you, who alone are good, the source of life,
have made all that is,
so that you might fill your creatures with blessings
and bring joy to many of them by the glory of your light.

And so, in your presence are countless hosts of Angels,
who serve you day and night
and, gazing upon the glory of your face,
glorify you without ceasing.

With them we, too, confess your name in exultation,

giving voice to every creature under heaven,
as we acclaim:
The people sing or say aloud the Sanctus as on page 70.

Pr. We give you praise, Father most holy,
for you are great
and you have fashioned all your works
in wisdom and in love.
You formed man in your own image
and entrusted the whole world to his care,
so that in serving you alone, the Creator,
he might have dominion over all creatures.
And when through disobedience he had lost your friendship,
you did not abandon him to the domain of death.
For you came in mercy to the aid of all,
so that those who seek might find you.
Time and again you offered them covenants
and through the prophets
taught them to look forward to salvation.

    And you so loved the world, Father most holy,
that in the fullness of time
you sent your Only Begotten Son to be our Saviour.
Made incarnate by the Holy Spirit
and born of the Virgin Mary,
he shared our human nature
in all things but sin.
To the poor he proclaimed the good news of salvation,

to prisoners, freedom,
and to the sorrowful of heart, joy.
To accomplish your plan,
he gave himself up to death,
and, rising from the dead,
he destroyed death and restored life.

And that we might live no longer for ourselves
but for him who died and rose again for us,
he sent the Holy Spirit from you, Father,
as the first fruits for those who believe,
so that, bringing to perfection his work in the world,
he might sanctify creation to the full.

Therefore, O Lord, we pray:
may this same Holy Spirit
graciously sanctify these offerings,
that they may become
the Body and ✠ Blood of our Lord Jesus Christ
for the celebration of this great mystery,
which he himself left us
as an eternal covenant.

For when the hour had come
for him to be glorified by you, Father most holy,
having loved his own who were in the world,
he loved them to the end:
and while they were at supper,
he took bread, blessed and broke it,
and gave it to his disciples, saying:

> 'Take this, all of you, and eat of it,
> for this is my Body,
> which will be given up for you.'

In a similar way,
taking the chalice filled with the fruit of the vine,
he gave thanks,
and gave the chalice to his disciples, saying:

> 'Take this, all of you, and drink from it,
> for this is the chalice of my Blood,
> the Blood of the new and eternal covenant,
> which will be poured out for you and for many
> for the forgiveness of sins.
> Do this in memory of me.'

Pr. The mystery of faith.
The people continue with one of the acclamations on page 74.

Pr. Therefore, O Lord,
as we now celebrate the memorial of our redemption,
we remember Christ's Death
and his descent to the realm of the dead,
we proclaim his Resurrection
and his Ascension to your right hand,
and, as we await his coming in glory,
we offer you his Body and Blood,
the sacrifice acceptable to you
which brings salvation to the whole world.

Look, O Lord, upon the Sacrifice
which you yourself have provided for your Church,
and grant in your loving kindness
to all who partake of this one Bread and one Chalice
that, gathered into one body by the Holy Spirit,
they may truly become a living sacrifice in Christ
to the praise of your glory.

Therefore, Lord, remember now
all for whom we offer this sacrifice:
especially your servant N. our Pope,
N. our Bishop,* and the whole Order of Bishops,
all the clergy,
those who take part in this offering,
those gathered here before you,
your entire people,
and all who seek you with a sincere heart.

Remember also
those who have died in the peace of your Christ
and all the dead,
whose faith you alone have known.

To all of us, your children,
grant, O merciful Father,
that we may enter into a heavenly inheritance
with the Blessed Virgin Mary, Mother of God,
with blessed Joseph, her Spouse,
and with your Apostles and Saints in your kingdom.
There, with the whole of creation,

---

* Mention may be made here of the Coadjutor Bishop, or Auxiliary Bishops.

freed from the corruption of sin and death,
may we glorify you through Christ our Lord,
through whom you bestow on the world all that is good.
The Priest takes the chalice and the paten with the host:
Through him, and with him, and in him,
O God, almighty Father,
in the unity of the Holy Spirit,
all glory and honour is yours,
for ever and ever. **R. Amen.**

The Communion Rite

Eating and drinking together the Lord's Body and Blood in a paschal meal is the culmination of the Eucharist.

The Lord's Prayer

After the chalice and paten have been set down, the congregation stands and the Priest says:
Pr. At the Saviour's command
and formed by divine teaching,
we dare to say:
Pr. Præceptis salutáribus móniti,
et divína institutióne formati,
audémus dicere:

Together with the people, he continues:
**Our Father, who art in heaven,
hallowed be thy name;
thy kingdom come,**

**thy will be done
on earth as it is in heaven.
Give us this day our daily bread,
and forgive us our trespasses,
as we forgive those who trespass against us;
and lead us not into temptation,
but deliver us from evil.**

Pater noster, qui es in cælis;
sanctificétur nomen tuum;
advéniat regnum tuum;
fiat voluntas tua sicut in cælo, et in terra.
Pancm nostrum cotidiánum da nobis hódie;
et dimítte nobis débita nostra,
sicut et nos dimíttimus debitóribus nostris;
et ne nos indúcas in tentatiónem;
sed líbera nos a malo.

Pr. Deliver us, Lord, we pray, from every evil,
graciously grant peace in our days,
that, by the help of your mercy,
we may be always free from sin
and safe from all distress,
as we await the blessed hope
and the coming of our Saviour, Jesus Christ.
**R. For the kingdom,
the power and the glory are yours
now and for ever.**

The Peace

Pr. Lord Jesus Christ,
who said to your Apostles:
Peace I leave you, my peace I give you;
look not on our sins,
but on the faith of your Church,
and graciously grant her peace and unity
in accordance with your will.
Who live and reign for ever and ever.
R. Amen.
Pr. The peace of the Lord be with you always.
R. And with your spirit.

Then the Deacon, or the Priest, adds:
Pr. Let us offer each other the sign of peace.
And all offer one another the customary sign of peace.

Breaking of the Bread

Then the Priest takes the host, breaks it over the paten, and places a small piece in the chalice, saying quietly:
Pr. May this mingling of the Body and Blood
of our Lord Jesus Christ
bring eternal life to us who receive it.
Meanwhile the following is sung or said:

**Lamb of God, you take away the sins of the world,
have mercy on us.
Lamb of God, you take away the sins of the world,
have mercy on us.
Lamb of God, you take away the sins of the world,
grant us peace.**

Agnus Dei, qui tollis peccáta mundi:
miserére nobis.

Agnus Dei, qui tollis peccáta mundi:
miserére nobis.

Agnus Dei, qui tollis peccáta mundi:
dona nobis pacem.

Invitation to Communion

All kneel; The Priest genuflects, takes the host and, holding it slightly raised above the paten or above the chalice says aloud:

Pr. Behold the Lamb of God,
behold him who takes away the sins of the world.
Blessed are those called to the supper of the Lamb.

**R. Lord, I am not worthy
that you should enter under my roof,
but only say the word
and my soul shall be healed.**

*While the Priest is receiving the Body of Christ,
the Communion Chant begins.*

Communion Procession

After the priest has reverently consumed the Body and Blood of Christ he takes the paten or ciborium and approaches the communicants.

The Priest raises a host slightly and shows it to each of the communicants, saying:

Pr. The Body of Christ.

R. Amen.

When Communion is ministered from the chalice:

Pr. The Blood of Christ.

R. Amen.

After the distribution of Communion, if appropriate, a sacred silence may be observed for a while, or a psalm or other canticle of praise or a hymn may be sung. Then, the Priest says:

Pr. Let us pray.

Prayer after Communion

All stand and pray in silence for a while, unless silence has just been observed. Then the Priest says the Prayer after Communion, at the end of which the people acclaim:

R. Amen.

The Order of Mass

The Concluding Rites

The Mass closes, sending the faithful forth to put what they have celebrated into effect in their daily lives.

Any brief announcements follow here. Then the dismissal takes place.

Pr. The Lord be with you.
R. And with your spirit.

The Priest blesses the people, saying:
Pr. May almighty God bless you,
the Father, and the Son, ✠ and the Holy Spirit.
R. Amen.

Then the Deacon, or the Priest himself says the Dismissal:
Pr. Go forth, the Mass is ended.
R. Thanks be to God. *Or:*
Pr. Go and announce the Gospel of the Lord.
R. Thanks be to God. *Or:*
Pr. Go in peace, glorifying the Lord by your life.
R. Thanks be to God. *Or:*
Pr. Go in peace.
R. Thanks be to God.

Then the Priest venerates the altar as at the beginning. After making a profound bow with the ministers, he withdraws.

If You Cannot Attend Mass

Spiritual Communion

Spiritual Communion is the heartfelt desire to receive Our Lord, even when we are unable because of the distance or for some other reason. This desire to receive him through spiritual Communion is an act of love which prolongs our thanksgiving even when we are not in the Eucharistic presence of Our Lord. The wish to live constantly in his presence can be fuelled by acts of love and desire to be united with him and is a means of drawing more deeply from the life of the Holy Spirit dwelling within our souls in the state of grace. 'The effects of a sacrament can be received by desire. Although in such a case the sacrament is not received physically ... nevertheless the actual reception of the sacrament itself brings with it fuller effect than receiving it through desire alone (St Thomas Aquinas). The writings of the saints reveal many formulae for making a spiritual Communion:

Acts of Spiritual Communion

My Jesus, I believe that You are truly present in the Most Holy Sacrament. I love You above all things, and I desire to receive You into my soul. Since I cannot at this moment

If You Cannot Attend Mass

receive You sacramentally, come at least spiritually into my heart. I embrace You as being already there and unite myself wholly to You. Never permit me to be separated from You. Amen.
(*St Alphonsus Liguori*)

I wish, my Lord, to receive You with the purity, humility and devotion with which Your Most Holy Mother received You, with the spirit and fervour of the saints.

Come Lord Jesus.

Give me, good Lord, a longing to be with You … give me warmth, delight and quickness in thinking upon You. And give me Your grace to long for Your holy sacraments, and specially to rejoice in the presence of Your very blessed Body, Sweet Saviour Christ, in the Holy Sacrament of the altar. (*St Thomas More*)

— Prayers for Holy Communion —

Say these Prayers slowly, a few words at a time. It is well to stop after every few words, that they may sink into the heart. Each Prayer may be said several times.

Prayer before Mass

O God, to whom every heart is open, every desire known and from whom no secrets are hidden; purify the thoughts of our hearts by the inspiration of your Holy Spirit, that we may perfectly love you, and worthily praise your holy name. Amen.

Before Holy Communion

Prayer for Help

O God, help me to make a good Communion. Mary, my dearest mother, pray to Jesus for me. My dear Angel Guardian, lead me to the Altar of God.

Act of Faith

O God, because you have said it, I believe that I shall receive the Sacred Body of Jesus Christ to eat, and his Precious Blood to drink. My God, I believe this with all my heart.

Act of Humility

My God, I confess that I am a poor sinner; I am not worthy to receive the Body and Blood of Jesus, on account of my sins. Lord, I am not worthy to receive you under my roof; but only say the word, and my soul will be healed.

Act of Sorrow

My God, I detest all the sins of my life. I am sorry for them, because they have offended you, my God, you who are so good. I resolve never to commit sin any more. My good God, pity me, have mercy on me, forgive me.

Act of Adoration

O Jesus, great God, present on the Altar, I bow down before you. I adore you.

Act of Love and Desire

Jesus, I love you. I desire with all my heart to receive you. Jesus, come into my poor soul, and give me your Flesh to eat and your Blood to drink. Give me your whole Self, Body, Blood, Soul and Divinity, that I may live for ever with you.

Prayer of St Thomas Aquinas

Almighty and ever-living God, I approach the sacrament of your only-begotten Son, our Lord Jesus Christ. I come sick to the doctor of life, unclean to the fountain of mercy, blind to the radiance of eternal light, poor and needy to the Lord of heaven and earth. Lord in your great generosity, heal my sickness, wash away my defilement, enlighten my blindness, enrich my poverty, and clothe my nakedness. May I receive the bread of angels, the King of kings and Lord of lords, with humble reverence, with purity and faith, with repentance and love and the determined purpose that will help to bring me to salvation. May I receive the sacrament of the Lord's body and blood and its reality and power. Kind God, may I receive the body of your only begotten Son, our Lord Jesus Christ, born from the womb of the Virgin Mary, and so be received into his mystical body and numbered among his members. Loving Father, as on my earthly pilgrimage I now receive your beloved Son under the veil of a sacrament, may I one day see him face to face in glory, who lives and reigns with you for ever. Amen.

Receiving Holy Communion

When the priest or minister says "The Body of Christ", answer "Amen" *and receive the sacred host with reverence.* If you receive *Holy Communion in the hand,* place the host *reverently into your mouth before returning to your place. If Holy Communion is given from the chalice, answer* "Amen" *when the priest or minister says* "The Blood of Christ"; *take the chalice and drink a little of the Precious Blood, taking care not to spill any. Say in your heart, with all the faith of St Thomas* "My Lord and my God". *Jesus is now really present in you. Keep away all earthly thoughts and enjoy his presence.*

AFTER HOLY COMMUNION

I give you thanks

I give you thanks, Lord, Holy Father, everlasting God. In your great mercy, and not because of my own merits, you have fed me a sinner and your unworthy servant, with the Precious Body and Blood of your Son, our Lord Jesus Christ. I pray that this Holy Communion may not serve as my judgement and condemnation, but as my forgiveness and salvation. May it be my armour of faith and shield of good purpose, root out in me all that is evil and increase every virtue. I beseech you to bring me a sinner, to that great feast where, with your Son and the Holy Spirit you are the true light of your holy ones, their flawless blessedness, everlasting joy and perfect happiness. Through Christ our Lord. Amen. (*St Thomas Aquinas*)

Act of Faith

O Jesus, I believe that I have received your Flesh to eat and your Blood to drink, because you have said it, and your word is true. All that I have and all that I am are your gift and now you have given me yourself.

Act of Adoration

O Jesus, my God, my Creator, I adore you, because from your hands I came and with you I am to be happy for ever.

Act of Humility

O Jesus, I am not worthy to receive you, and yet you have come to me that my poor heart may learn of you to be meek and humble.

Act of Love

Jesus, I love you; I love you with all my heart. You know that I love you, and wish to love you daily more and more.

Act of Thanksgiving

My good Jesus, I thank you with all my heart. How good, how kind you are to me. Blessed be Jesus in the most holy Sacrament of the Altar.

Act of Offering

O Jesus, receive my poor offering.
Jesus, you have given yourself to me,

and now let me give myself to you:
I give you my body, that I may be chaste and pure.
I give you my soul, that I may be free from sin.
I give you my heart, that I may always love you.
I give you my every breath that I shall breathe,
and especially my last.
I give you myself in life and in death,
that I may be yours for ever and ever.

For Yourself

O Jesus, wash away my sins with your Precious Blood.
O Jesus, the struggle against temptation is not yet finished. My Jesus, when temptation comes near me, make me strong against it. In the moment of temptation may I always say: "My Jesus, mercy! Mary, help!"
O Jesus, may I lead a good life; may I die a happy death. May I receive you before I die. May I say when I am dying: "Jesus, Mary and Joseph, I give you my heart and my soul".
Listen now for a moment to Jesus Christ; perhaps he has something to say to you. Answer Jesus in your heart, and tell him all your troubles. Then say:

For Perseverance

Jesus, I am going away for a time, but I trust not without you. You are with me by your grace. I resolve never to leave you by mortal sin. Although I am so weak I have such hope in you. Give me grace to persevere. Amen.

Rite of Eucharistic
Exposition and Benediction

The service of Benediction developed during the Middle Ages during the Corpus Christi processions in which the Blessed Sacrament was held up for veneration. The service was subsequently used at other times throughout the year as an opportunity to give thanks for the Mass and adore Christ present under the form of bread.

Today, the Church encourages this rite to be celebrated in the context of a longer period of reading, prayer and reflection.

Exposition

First of all, the minister exposes the Blessed Sacrament while a hymn is sung, during which he incenses the Sacrament. The following or another hymn may be chosen.

O salutáris hóstia, Quæ cæli pandis óstium; Bella premunt hostília, Da robur, fer auxílium.	O saving Victim, opening wide / The gate of heaven to man below / Our foes press on from every side / Thine aid supply, thy strength bestow.

Uni Trinóque Dómino Sit sempitérna glória, Qui vitam sine término Nobis donet in pátria.
Amen.

To thy great name be endless praise / Immortal Godhead, One in Three / O grant us endless length of days / In our true native land with thee. **Amen.**

ADORATION

A time for silent prayer, readings from Scripture, litanies or other prayers and hymns. On some occasions, the Prayer of the Church might be said or sung.

BENEDICTION

Towards the end of the exposition, the priest or deacon goes to the altar, genuflects and kneels. Then this hymn or a suitable alternative is sung, during which the minister incenses the sacrament.

Tantum ergo Sacraméntum Venerémur cérnui:

Et antíquum documéntum Novo cedat rítui:

Præstet fides suppleméntum Sénsuum deféctui.

Therefore we, before him bending / This great Sacrament revere / Types and shadows have their ending / for the newer rite is here / Faith, our outward sense befriending / Makes the inward vision clear.

Genitóri, Genitóque,	Glory let us give, and blessing / To the Father and the Son / Honour, might, and praise addressing / While eternal ages run / Ever too his love confessing / Who, from both, with both is one.
Laus et iubilátio.	
Salus, honor, virtus quoque	
Sit et benedíctio;	
Procedénti ab utróque;	
Compar sit laudátio.	
Amen.	**Amen.**

The traditional responsory may be used:

V. Panem de cælo præstitisti eis (alleluia)
R. Omne delectamentum in se habentem (alleluia)
V. You gave them bread from heaven (alleluia)
R. Containing in itself all goodness (alleluia)

The minister then says the following prayer (or a suitable alternative)

Lord Jesus Christ,
You gave us the Eucharist
As the memorial of your suffering and death.
May our worship of this Sacrament
Of your Body and Blood
Help us to experience the salvation
You won for us
And the peace of the kingdom

Where you live with the Father
And the Holy Spirit,
One God, for ever and ever. **Amen.**

The priest or deacon now puts on the humeral veil and blesses the congregation with the Blessed Sacrament.

The Divine Praises formerly said at this point may more properly be included within the period of adoration.

The Divine Praises

Blessed be God.
Blessed be his holy Name.
Blessed be Jesus Christ, true God and true Man.
Blessed be the name of Jesus.
Blessed be his most Sacred Heart.
Blessed be his most Precious Blood.
Blessed be Jesus in the most holy Sacrament of the Altar.
Blessed be the Holy Spirit, the Paraclete.
Blessed be the great Mother of God, Mary most holy.
Blessed be her holy and Immaculate Conception.
Blessed be her glorious Assumption.
Blessed be the name of Mary, Virgin and Mother.
Blessed be Saint Joseph, her spouse most chaste.
Blessed be God in his Angels and in his Saints.

REPOSITION

Immediately after the Blessed Sacrament is reposed in the tabernacle, the following may be sung

Ant. Adorémus in ætérnum sanctíssimum Sacraméntum.

Ant. Let us adore for ever the most holy Sacrament.

Ps. Laudáte Dóminum, omnes gentes; laudáte eum omnes pópuli. Quóniam confirmáta est super nos misericórdia ejus, et véritas Dómini manet in ætérnum.

Ps. O praise the Lord, all you nations / Acclaim him, all you peoples / For his mercy is confirmed upon us / and the truth of the Lord remains for ever.

Glória Patri, et Filio, et Spirítui Sancto. Sicut erat in princípio, et nunc, et semper, et in sáecula sæculórum. **Amen.**

Glory be to the Father, and to the Son / and to the Holy Spirit / As it was in the beginning, is now / and ever shall be, world without end. **Amen.**

Ant. Adorémus in ætérnum sanctíssimum Sacraméntum.

Ant. Let us adore for ever the most holy Sacrament.

An alternative acclamation:
O Sacrament most holy, O Sacrament divine!
All praise, and all thanksgiving,
Be every moment thine!

A Quarter of an Hour Before The Blessed Sacrament

Sitting or kneeling before Jesus truly present in the Blessed Sacrament, it may be helpful to reflect on the love and tenderness of our Lord, by meditating upon this text:

To please Me, dear child, it is not necessary to know much; all that is required is to love Me much, to be deeply sorry for ever having offended Me and desirous of being ever faithful to Me in future.

Speak to Me now as you would do to your dearest friend. Tell Me all that now fills your mind and heart. Are there any you wish to commend to Me? Tell Me their names, and tell Me what you would wish Me to do for them. Do not fear, ask for much; I love generous hearts, which, forgetting themselves, wish well to others.

Speak to Me of the poor you wish to comfort; tell Me of the sick that you would wish to see relieved. Ask of Me something for those who have been unkind to you, or who have crossed you. Ask much for them all; commend them with all your heart to Me.

And ask Me many graces for yourself. Are there not many graces you would wish to name that would make you happier in yourself, more useful and pleasing to others, more worthy of the love of Me, the dearest Lord, Master, and Spouse of your soul? Tell Me the whole list of the favours you want of Me. Tell Me them with humility, knowing how poor you are without them, how unable to gain them by yourself; ask for them with much love, that they may make you more pleasing to Me. With all a child's simplicity, tell Me how self-seeking you are, how proud, vain, irritable, how cowardly in sacrifice, how lazy in work, uncertain in your good resolutions, and then ask Me to bless and crown your efforts. Poor child, fear not, blush not at the sight of so many failings; there are Saints in heaven who had the faults you have; they came to Me lovingly, they prayed earnestly to Me, and My grace has made them good and holy in My sight.

You should be Mine, body and soul; fear not, therefore, to ask of Me gifts of body and mind, health, judgment, memory, and success – ask for them for My sake; that God may be glorified in all things. I can grant everything, and never refuse to give what may make a soul dearer to Me and better able to fulfil the will of God. Have you no plans for the future which occupy, perhaps distress, your mind? Tell Me your hopes, your fears. Is it about your future state? Your position among My creatures? Some good you wish to bring to others? In what shall I help and bless your good will?

And for Me you must have – have you not? – some zeal, some wish to do good to the souls of others. Some, perhaps, who love and care for you, have ceased, almost, to know or care for Me. Shall I give you strength, wisdom and tact, to bring these poor ones close to My heart again? Have you failed in the past? Tell me how you acted; I will show you why you did not gain all you expected; rely on Me, I will help you, and will guide you to lead others to Me.

And what crosses have you, My dear child? Have they been many and heavy ones? Has someone caused you pain? Someone wounded your self-love? slighted you? injured you? Lay your head upon My breast, and tell Me how you suffered. Have you felt that some have been ungrateful to you, and unfeeling towards you? Tell Me all, and in the warmth of My heart you will find strength to forgive and even to forget that they have ever wished to pain you.

And what fears have you, my child? My providence shall comfort you. My love sustain you. I am never away from you, never can abandon you. Are some growing cold in the interest and love they had for you? Pray to Me for them; I will restore them to you if it be better for you and your sanctification.

Have you got some happiness to make known to Me? What happened since you came to Me last, to console you, to gladden and give you joy? What was it? a mark of true friendship you received? a success unexpected and almost unhoped for? a fear suddenly taken away from you? and did you remember the while, that in all it was My will,

My love, that brought all that your heart has been so glad to have? It was My hand, My dear child, that guided and prepared all for you. Look to Me now, My child, and say: 'Dear Jesus, I thank you'.

You will soon leave Me now; what promises can you make me? Let them be sincere ones, humble ones, full of love and desire to please Me. Tell Me how carefully you will avoid every occasion of sin, drive from you all that leads to harm, and shun the world – the great deceiver of souls. Promise to be kind to the poor; loving, for My sake, to friends; forgiving to your enemies, and charitable to all, not in word alone and actions, but in your very thoughts. When you have little love for your neighbour, whom you see, you are forgetting Me who am hidden from you.

Love all my Saints; seek the help of your holy patrons. I love to glorify them by giving you much through them. Love, above all, My own sweet glorious Mother – she is your mother; love her, speak to her often, and she will bring you to Me, and for her sake, I will love and bless you more each day.

Return soon to Me again, but come with your heart empty of the world, for I have many more favours to give, more than you can know of; bring your heart so that I may fill it with many gifts of My love.

My peace be with you.

CATHOLIC TEACHING
– Summary of Christian Doctrine –

Reference to the *Catechism of the Catholic Church*, which is an "organic presentation of the Catholic faith in its entirety", can enrich this brief summary (*Catechism* 18).

1. We believe that the existence of God can be known with certainty by the natural light of human reason. God revealed himself to us as a personal and loving God. We believe that God is one God in three persons, the Father, the Son and the Holy Spirit. God the Son, the second person of the Blessed Trinity, was made man, died upon the Cross to save us and rose triumphant from the dead. We believe that the human person is created body and soul with free will. God wills every person to be saved for eternal life in the Kingdom of heaven. It is possible for us to reject God through sin and be separated from him forever in hell.

2. We believe all that is contained in the Creed. The Creed is divided into three parts: "the first part speaks of the first divine Person and the wonderful work of creation; the next speaks of the second divine Person and the mystery of his redemption of men; the final part speaks of the third divine Person, the origin and source of our sanctification" (*Catechism* 190).

3. Jesus Christ founded the Church to continue his teaching and sanctifying work on earth until the end of time. "In order to preserve the Church in the purity of the faith handed on by the apostles, Christ who is the Truth willed to confer on her a share in his own infallibility" (*Catechism* 889). Mindful of the words of Christ "he who hears you hears me" (*Luke* 10:16), we believe what the Church teaches us in matters of faith and morals.

The Ten Commandments of God

The Ten Commandments are a privileged expression of the natural law. This law is made known to us by divine revelation and by human reason (*Catechism* 2070).

1. I am the Lord your God: you shall not have strange gods before me.
2. You shall not take the name of the Lord your God in vain.
3. Remember to keep holy the Lord's day.
4. Honour your father and your mother.
5. You shall not kill.
6. You shall not commit adultery.
7. You shall not steal.
8. You shall not bear false witness against your neighbour.
9. You shall not covet your neighbour's wife.
10. You shall not covet your neighbour's goods.

The Seven Sacraments

The seven sacraments are outward signs of inward grace, given by Jesus Christ. "Celebrated worthily in faith, the sacraments confer the grace that they signify. They are efficacious because in them Christ himself is at work" (*Catechism* 1127).

1. *Baptism***:** by which we are made Christians, children of God, members of his holy Church, and heirs of heaven.

2. *Confirmation***:** by which we receive the Holy Spirit, to make us strong and perfect Christians, and soldiers of Christ.

3. *The Holy Eucharist***:** which is really and truly and substantially the Body and Blood, the Soul and Divinity, of Jesus Christ, under the appearances of bread and wine. The Holy Eucharist is not only a Sacrament, in which we receive our divine Lord for the food and nourishment of our souls, and in which he is really present to be adored upon the altar; it is also a Sacrifice, the Sacrifice of the Holy Mass, in which, at the time of consecration, the bread and wine are changed into the Body and Blood of Jesus Christ, and in which he is offered up for us to his eternal Father.

4. *Penance***:** by which the sins committed after Baptism are forgiven.

5. *Anointing of the Sick*: which, in dangerous illness, and in preparation for death, comforts the soul, remits sins, and restores health if God sees this to be expedient.

6. *Holy Orders*: by which Bishops, Priests, and Deacons receive power and grace to perform their sacred duties.

7. *Matrimony*: which is the Sacrament of Christian Marriage.

The Six Chief Commandments of the Church

1. To keep the Sundays and holy days of Obligation holy, by hearing Mass and resting from servile works.
2. To keep the days of Fasting and Abstinence appointed by the Church.
3. To go to Confession when we are conscious of having sinned gravely.
4. To receive the Blessed Sacrament at least once a year, at Easter or thereabouts.
5. To contribute to the support of our pastors.
6. Not to marry within certain degrees of kindred without dispensation.

The Three Theological Virtues

Faith, Hope, and Charity.

Catholic Teaching

The Four Cardinal Virtues

Prudence, Justice, Fortitude, and Temperance.

The Seven gifts of the Holy Spirit

Wisdom, Understanding, Right Judgement, Courage, Knowledge, Reverence, the Spirit of Wonder and Awe in the presence of God.

The Twelve fruits of the Holy Spirit

Charity, Joy, Peace, Patience, Goodness, Kindness, Long-suffering, Mildness, Faith, Modesty, Self-control, Chastity.

The Seven Corporal Works of Mercy

To feed the hungry; to give drink to the thirsty; to clothe the naked; to harbour the harbourless; the visit the sick; to visit the imprisoned; to bury the dead.

The Seven Spiritual Works of Mercy

To counsel the doubtful; to instruct the ignorant; to admonish sinners; to comfort the afflicted; to forgive offences; to bear wrongs patiently; to pray for the living and the dead.

The Seven Deadly Sins and Opposite Virtues

Pride, Avarice, Lust, Anger, Gluttony, Envy, Sloth. Humility, Liberality, Chastity, Meekness, Temperance, Brotherly Love, Diligence.

The Mass Simply Explained

"At the Last Supper, on the night he was betrayed, our Saviour instituted the Eucharistic sacrifice of his Body and Blood. This he did in order to perpetuate the sacrifice of the cross throughout the ages until he should come again, and so to entrust to his beloved Spouse, the Church, a memorial of his death and resurrection: a sacrament of love, a sign of unity, a bond of charity, a Paschal banquet 'in which Christ is consumed, the mind is filled with grace, and a pledge of future glory is given to us'" (*Catechism* 1323).

First we come together in one place to celebrate the Eucharist in communion with the whole Church. At our head is Christ, the High Priest. The Bishop or priest acts in the person of Christ.

The word of God in the inspired scriptures is proclaimed. The homily encourages us to accept this word and to put it into practice. In the intercessions, we pray for the Church, for the world, for those in need and for local needs.

The offerings of bread and wine are placed upon the altar and offered by the priest in the name of Christ. The Creator's gifts are placed into the hands of Christ who, in his sacrifice perfects all human attempts to offer sacrifice.

The Eucharistic Prayer is the heart and summit of the whole celebration. The priest gives thanks to God in the preface and we praise him in union with the angels and saints. The priest asks the Father to send the Holy Spirit upon the gifts of bread and wine so that they truly become the Body and Blood of Jesus Christ. His one, eternal sacrifice offered for us upon the cross is made present. The Church calls to mind the passion, death and resurrection of Christ, which are made present in the Eucharist. The prayer reminds us that we offer the Eucharist in communion with the Bishop of Rome, the local Bishop and the whole Church throughout the world.

In Holy Communion, we share in the sacred and heavenly banquet and receive the body and blood of Christ as the "bread of heaven" and the "chalice of salvation", the food and life of our souls (*Catechism* 1346).

Who may receive Holy Communion

To receive Holy Communion, we must be "in communion" with the Church: we should be in a state of grace, keep the fast of one hour (not required for the elderly or sick), and we should prepare devoutly to receive the sacrament. The Church encourages those who are properly disposed to receive Holy Communion whenever they participate in the Mass.

Those who are living together as husband and wife but who are not married, or who are married outside the Church without permission may not receive Holy Communion.

If we are conscious of having committed a mortal sin, we should make a sacramental confession before receiving Holy Communion.

THE SUNDAY OBLIGATION

The first commandment of the Church binds all Catholics to attend Mass on all Sundays and Holy days of Obligation.

This is a grave obligation on our conscience, unless some really serious cause prevents us. To come in late, wilfully or through carelessness, when Mass has begun, is at least a venial sin. To miss Mass when you cannot help it, or when it would be very difficult for you to attend Mass, is not a sin. So, if you were to miss Mass because you were ill, or because you had to stay at home to mind a sick person or children, or because you were a very long way from church, or if for some other reason you could not go, it would not be a sin. When you cannot go to Mass, say the Mass prayers yourself at home, if possible. (*See page* 89, *above*).

FASTING AND ABSTINENCE

The age at which abstinence becomes binding is fourteen. The obligation of fasting is restricted to those who have completed their eighteenth year and it continues until they have begun their sixtieth.

Fasting and abstinence are binding throughout the Church on Ash Wednesday and Good Friday.

The law of the Church requires Catholics on Fridays to abstain from meat, or some other form of food, or to observe some form of penance laid down by the local Bishops' Conference. (*Code of Canon Law* 1251)

The Bishops of England and Wales have decided that in England and Wales this penance should be fulfilled simply by abstaining from meat and by uniting this to prayer. Those who cannot or choose not to eat meat as part of their normal diet should abstain from some other food of which they regularly partake.

The Eucharistic Fast

1. Water (and medicine) may be taken at any time.

2. Solid food and drinks may be taken up to one hour before Holy Communion.

3. Those who are advanced in age or who suffer from any infirmity, as well as those who take care of them, can receive Holy Communion even if they have taken something during the previous hour.

Note on Indulgences

An indulgence is a remission before God of the temporal punishment due to sins whose guilt has already been forgiven, which the faithful Christian who is duly disposed gains under certain prescribed conditions through the action of the Church which, as the minister of redemption, dispenses and applies with authority the treasury of the satisfactions of Christ and the saints. An indulgence is partial or plenary according as it removes either part or all of the temporal punishment due to sin. The faithful can gain indulgences for themselves or apply them to the dead. To understand this doctrine and practice of the Church, it is necessary to understand that sin has a double consequence. Grave sin deprives us of communion with God and therefore makes us incapable of eternal life, the privation of which is called the "eternal punishment" of sin. On the other hand every sin, even venial, entails an unhealthy attachment to creatures, which must be purified either here on earth, or after death in the state called Purgatory. This purification frees one from what is called the "temporal punishment" of sin. These two punishments must not be conceived of as a kind of vengeance inflicted by God from without, but as following from the very nature of sin (*Catechism* 1471-2).

Catholic Teaching

To gain a plenary indulgence it is necessary to perform the work to which the indulgence is attached and to fulfill the following three conditions:

- Sacramental Confession,
- Holy Communion,
- Prayer for the intention of the Holy Father.

It is further required that all attachment to sin, even venial sin, be absent. If this disposition is in any way less than perfect or if the prescribed three conditions are not fulfilled, the indulgence will be partial only.

The condition of praying for the intention of the Sovereign Pontiff is fully satisfied by reciting one Our Father and one Hail Mary; nevertheless, each one is free to recite any other prayer according to his piety and devotion.

A partial indulgence is granted to the faithful who:

1. In the performance of their duties and in bearing the trials of life, raise their mind with humble confidence to God, adding even if only mentally – some pious invocation.

2. In a spirit of faith and mercy give of themselves or of their goods to serve their brothers in need.

3. In a spirit of penance voluntarily deprive themselves of what is licit and pleasing to them.

For Specific prayers and devotions

The Holy Rosary (p.37): A plenary indulgence, for the recitation of the Rosary (five decades), in a church or public oratory or in the family. If said privately, a partial indulgence.

The Way of the Cross (p.31): A plenary indulgence.

Prayer before a Crucifix (p.51): A plenary indulgence, on the Fridays in Lent and Passiontide. At other times a partial indulgence.

Act of Resignation (p.42): A partial indulgence. A plenary indulgence at the hour of death, if properly disposed and the habit of reciting some prayers.

Helpful Reading

Morning and Evening Prayer

Psalms and Canticles (SC138)
Contemplative Meditation (D514)
A Guide to Morning and Evening Prayer (D671)
Morning and Evening Prayer: Meditations & Catechesis on the Psalms and Canticles (SC115)
The Gospel of Matthew (SC130)
The Gospel of Mark (SC131)
The Gospel of Luke (SC132)
The Gospel of John (SC133)

Penitential Prayers

A Simple Penance Book (D777)
Stations of the Cross: with St Alphonsus Ligouri (D799)

Prayers to Our Lady

33 Day Consecration to Jesus Through Mary (D793)
Marian Prayer Book (D752)
Novena to the Blessed Virgin Mary (D765)
Our Lady Untier of Knots (D769)
A Simple Rosary Book (D776)

Other Prayers and Devotions

The Divine Mercy (D650)
Devotion to the Sacred Heart (D643)
A Catholic Prayer Book (D778)

The Mass

The Order of Mass (in Latin and English) (D506)
The Holy Sacrifice of the Mass (DO963)
Is Jesus Really Present in the Eucharist? (DO727)
Eucharistic Adoration (D757)

Christian Doctrine

The Catechism of the Catholic Church (DO917)
Compendium of the Catechism of the Catholic Church (DO742)
Catholic Social Teaching (DO675)
A Catechism of Christian Doctrine (DO003)
What Catholics Believe (DO531)
Evangelium – Introduction to the Catholic Faith course (EV1-EV3)